Practice

Bothell, WA • Chicago, IL • Columbus, OH • New York, NY

Cover: Nathan Love

www.mheonline.com/readingwonderworks

Send all inquiries to:
McGraw-Hill Education
Two Penn Plaza
New York, New York 10121

ISBN: 978-0-02-129946-1
MHID: 0-02-129946-3

Printed in the United States of America.

4 5 6 7 8 9 QVS 18 17 16 15 14

A

CONTENTS

CONTENTS

Unit 3

Unit 4

Unit 5

Unit 6

CONTENTS

Unit 7

Unit 8

Unit 9

Unit 10

Name ______________________________

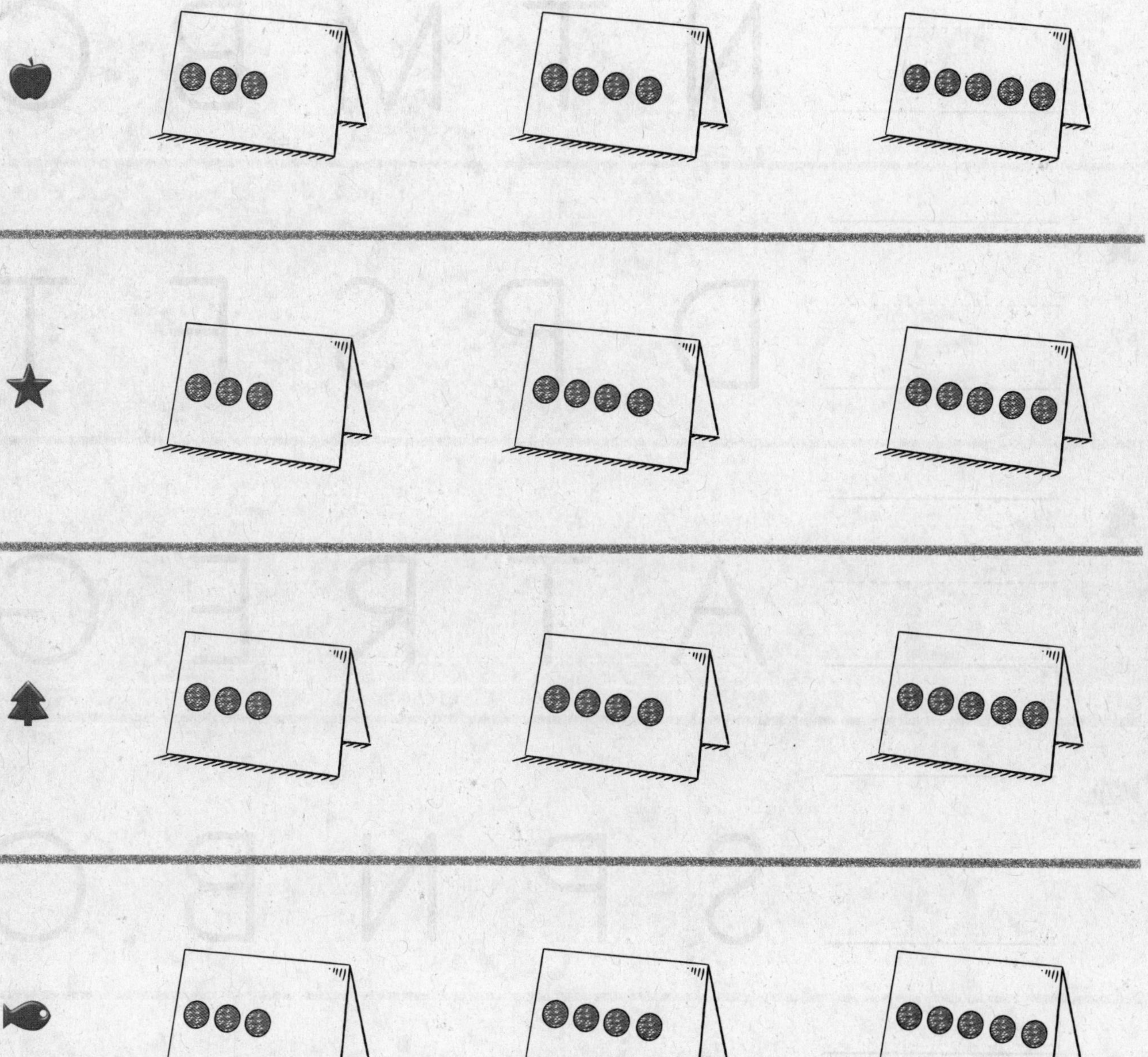

Phonological Awareness: Sentence Segmentation
Put your finger on the picture I say. Then listen as I say a sentence. Count the words in the sentence. Count the dots on each card. Circle the picture that shows the number of words in the sentence. Apple Row: *I can see the stars.* Star Row: *I like school.* Tree Row: *I can jump rope.* Fish Row: *My kitten is very soft.*

Name ______________________________

m N T M B C

s D P S F T

a A T R E G

p S P N B C

t H U C T W

Phonics: Letter recognition: Mm, Aa, Ss, Pp, Tt
Trace the lowercase letter at the beginning of each row and say its name. Then circle its partner
lCapital etter in the row.
in the row.

Name ______________________________

Ii	I	Tt	a
	B		b
i	C	T	t

Pp	a	Ss	S
	p		T
P	g	s	L

Mm	h	Ff	E
	m		F
M	b	f	Q

Phonics: Letter Recognition: Ff, Ii, Mm, Pp, Ss, Tt
Say the letter name. Trace the Capital and lowercase letters. Draw a line to match the letter at the bottom to its partner letter.

Name ______________________________

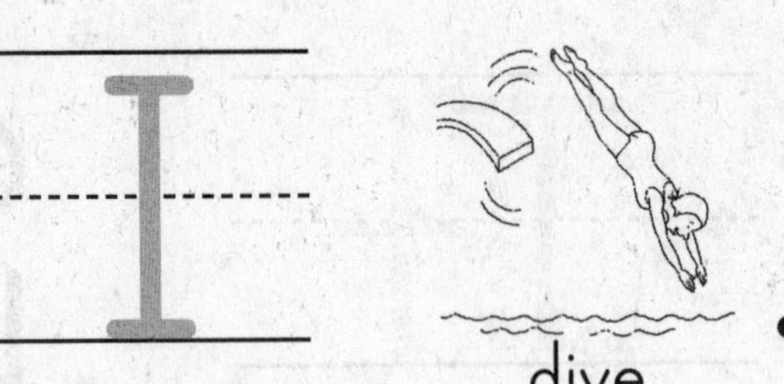

I dive.

I can swim.

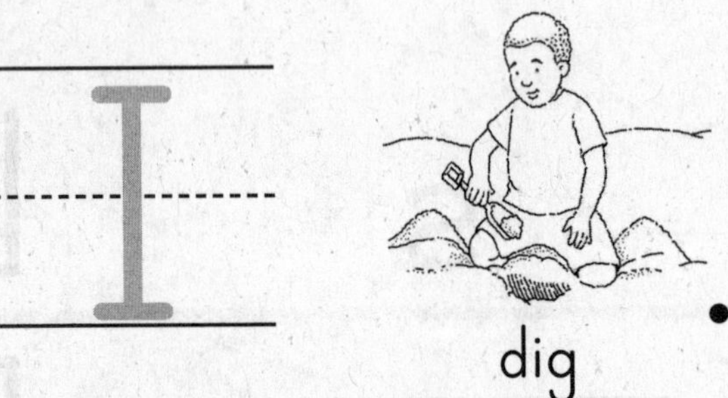

I dig.

I can build.

High-Frequency Words: ***I, can***
Say and trace the word in each sentence. Then read the sentence.

Name ____________________

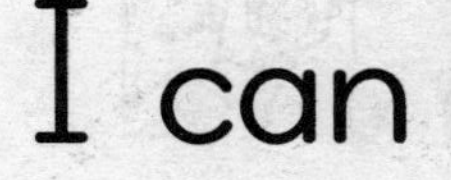

I can  .

sleep

I Can

I can [picture] .

sing

I can  .

swim

I can  .

swing

Name ______________________________

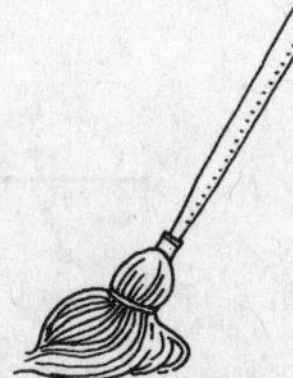

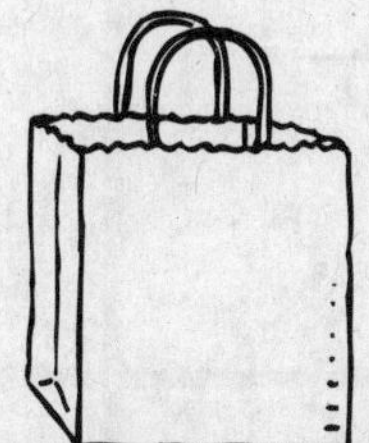

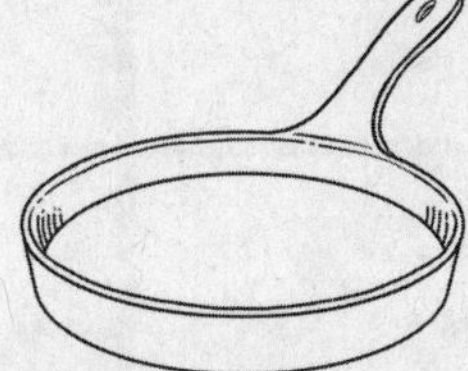

Phonemic Awareness: Phoneme Isolation

Listen to this word: *mix.* Listen for the beginning sound. /m/ /i/ /ks/. Now listen to each picture name: *mop, rug.* Circle the picture that has the same beginning sound as *mix.* ★ *tip* (*tub, bag*) *wish* (*sun, web*) *dig* (*duck, pan*); *nap* (*six, net*).

Name ____________________

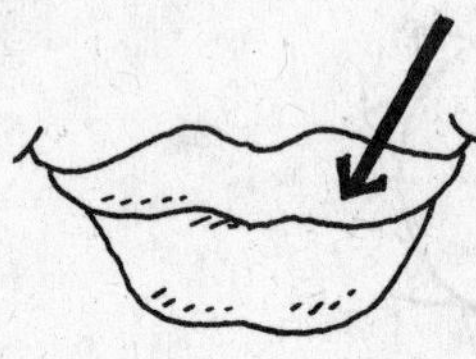

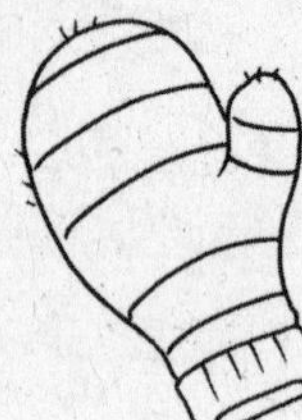

Phonics: initial *m*

Listen as I say each picture name. If the picture name begins with the /m/ sound, write *m* on the line. (*map, moon, duck, mouth, mitten*)

Name ______________________________

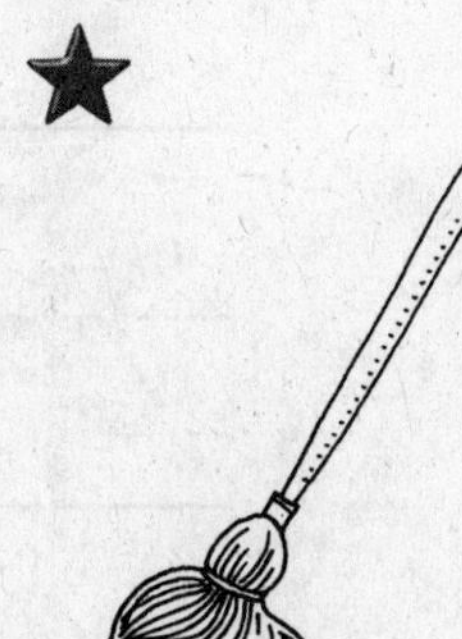

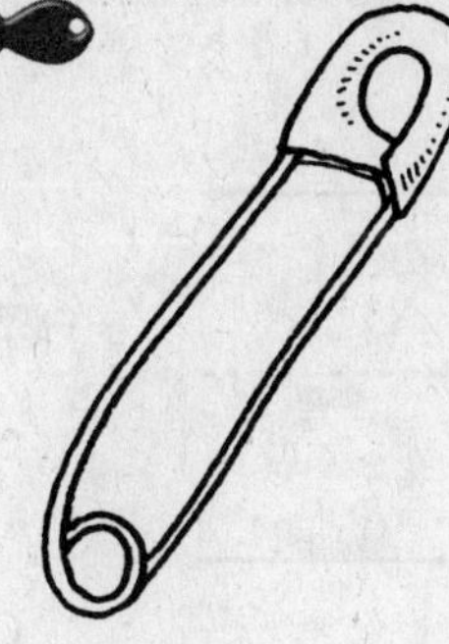

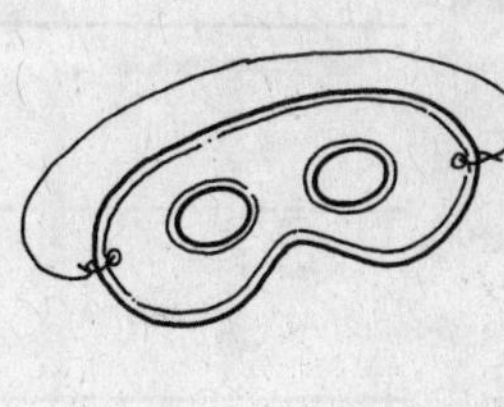

Phonics: initial *m*

Listen carefully as I say each picture name: *tent, mouse.* Circle the picture whose name begins with the /m/ sound. Write *m* on the line. (*mop, fork; sun, mirror; pin, mask*)

Name ______________________________

the

High-Frequency Words: ***the***
Say and trace the word *the* 🍎★🌲. Say and trace the word in each sentence. Read the sentence and draw a picture in the box to complete it.

Name ______________________

I can [see] the [duck].

see duck

I Can

I can [see] the [feathers].

see feathers

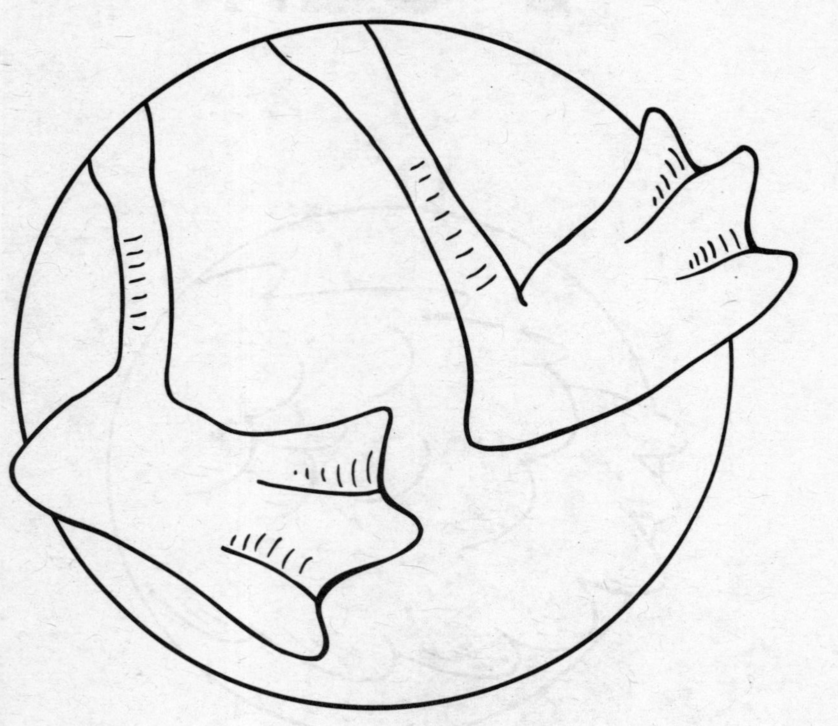

I can see the feet.

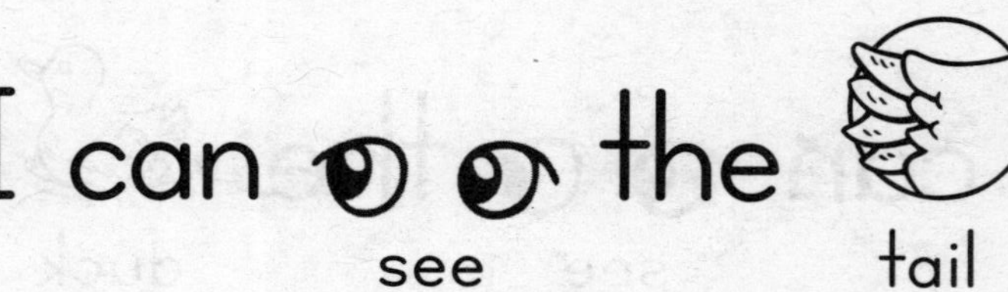

I can see the tail.

Name ______________________________

  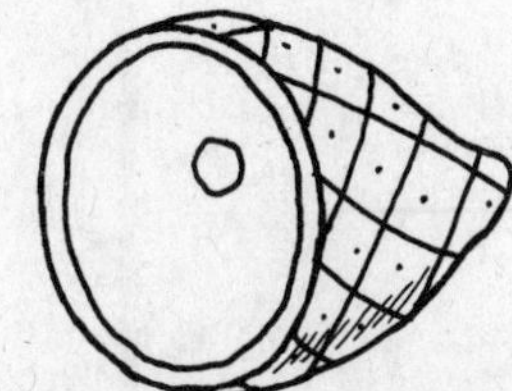

 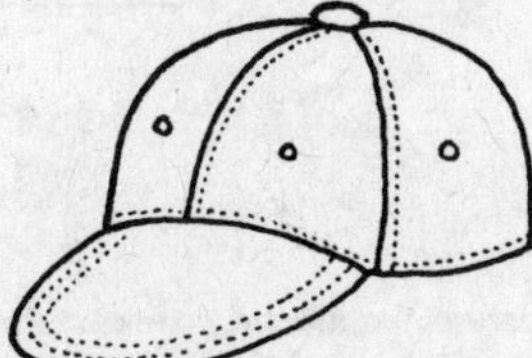 

  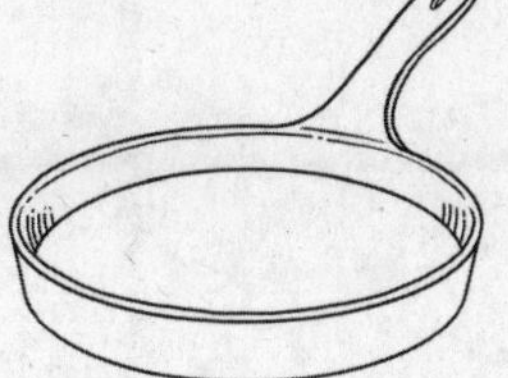

 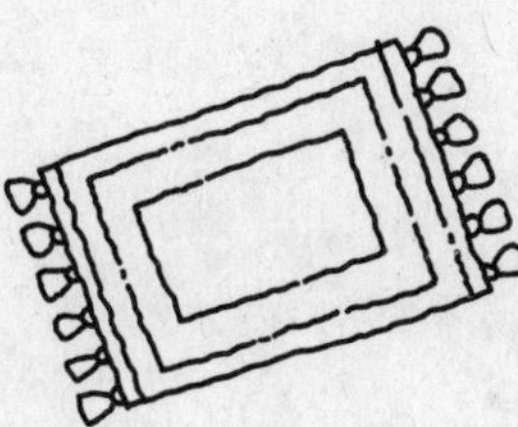 

Phonemic Awareness: Phoneme Isolation

Listen to this word: *sat.* Listen for the middle sound: /s/ /a/ /t/. Now listen to each picture name: *jet, ham.* Circle the picture that has the same middle sound as *sat.* ★ *rat* (*cap, pig*) *bat* (*tub, van*) *hop* (*fox, pan*); *nap* (*rug, bat*).

Name ______________________________

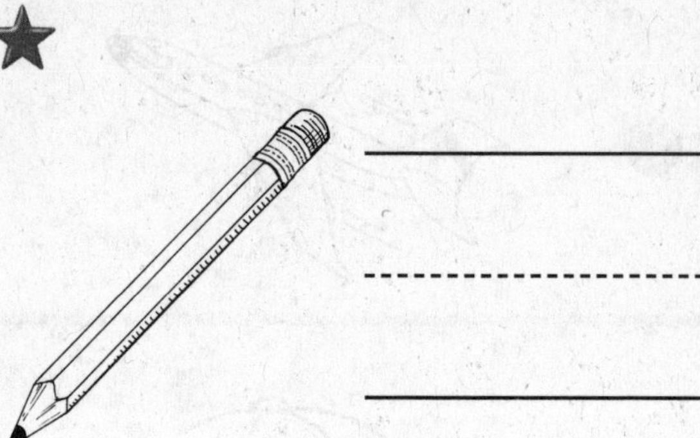

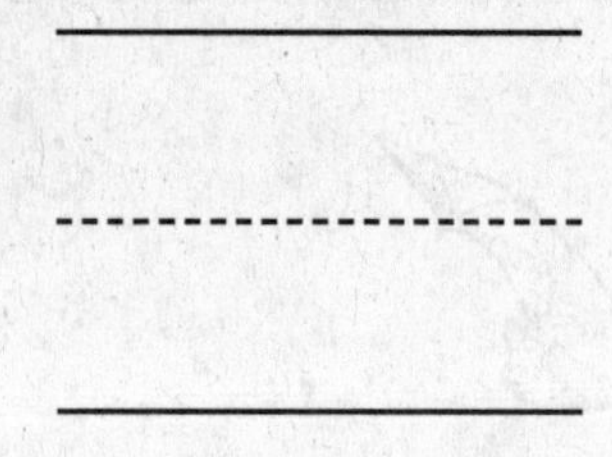

Phonics: initial short *a*
Listen as I say each picture name. If the picture name begins with the /a/ sound, write *a* on the line. (*ant, pencil, alligator, apple, astronaut*)

Name ______________________________

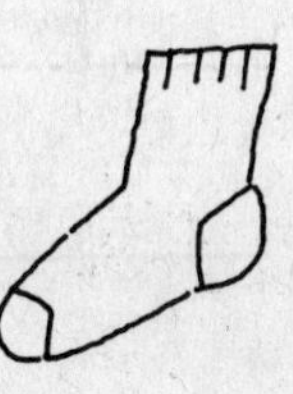

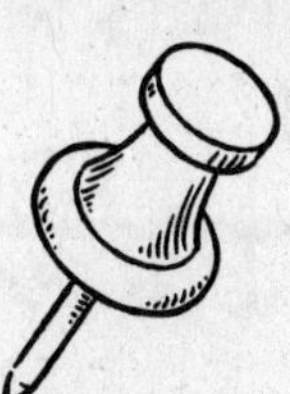

Phonics: medial short *a*

Listen carefully as I say each picture name: *fan, bug*. Circle the picture whose name has the /a/ sound in the middle. Write *a* on the line. (*gum, hat*; *cab, net*; *pad, sock*; *bib, tack*)

Name ______________________

 We  read .

 We 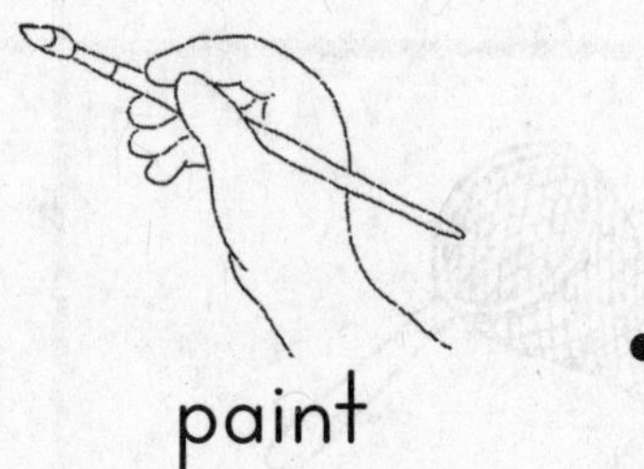 paint .

 We  sing .

 rest .

High-Frequency Words: ***we***
Say and trace the word in each sentence. Read the sentence.

Name ______________________________

We can see the snakes.

We Can

We can see the  tigers.

We can  the .

see turkeys

We can see the turtles.

Name ____

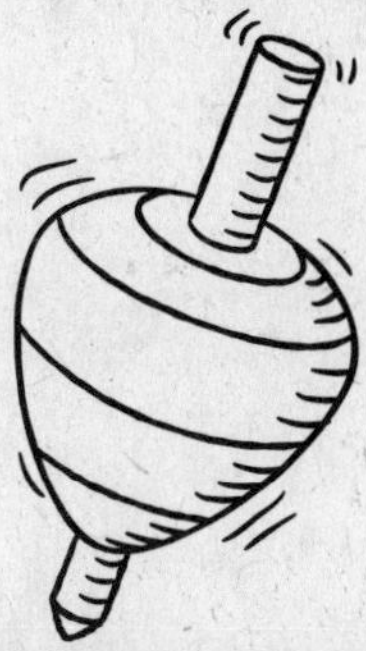

Phonemic Awareness: Phoneme Categorization

🍎 Listen to the beginning sound as I say each picture name: *sun, wig, sock*. Two words have the same beginning sound. Which word does not belong? Put an X on the picture whose name does not belong. ★ *top, monkey, mug;* 🌲 *ant, ax, can;* 🐟 *pen, rock, pig.*

Name ______________________________

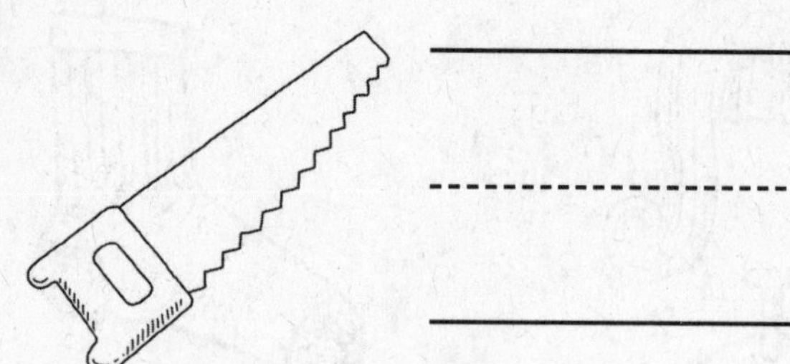

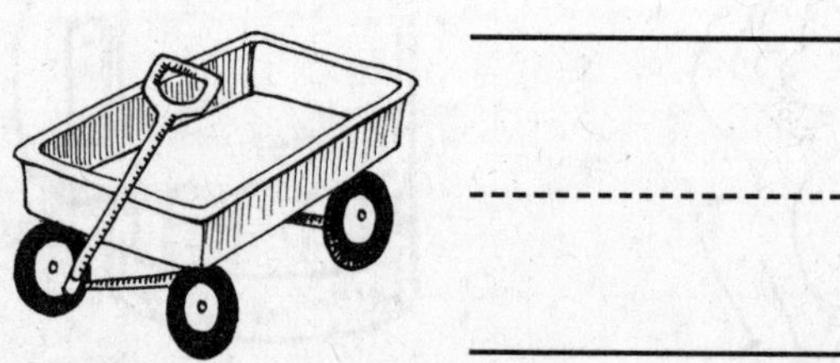

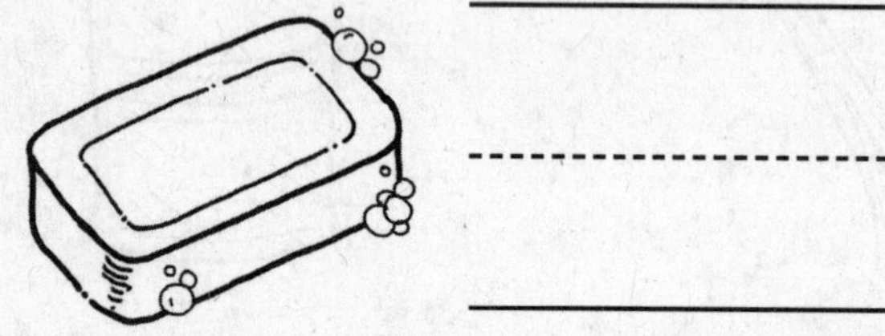

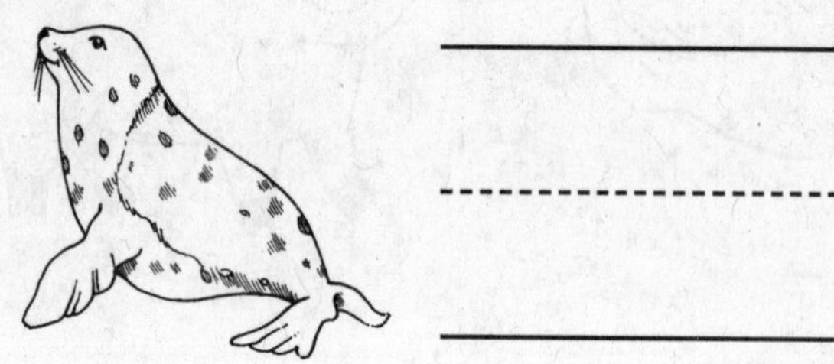

Phonics: initial *s*

Listen as I say each picture name. If the picture name begins with the /s/ sound, write *s* on the line. (*saw, wagon, soap, seal*)

Name ____________________

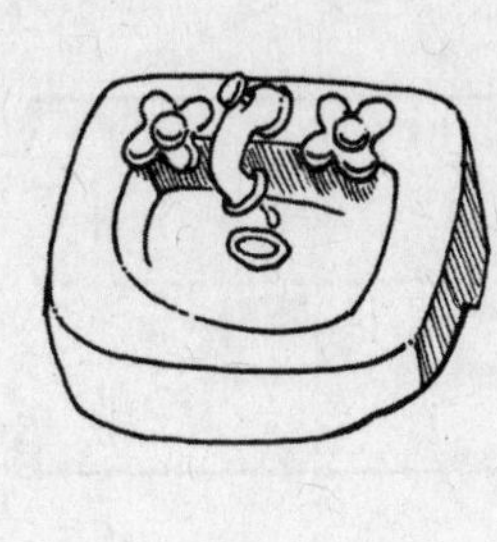

Phonics: initial *s*

Listen carefully as I say each picture name: *six, car.* Circle the picture whose name begins with the /s/ sound. Write *s* on the line. ★ *turkey, sail;* *sock, heart;* *sink, ant)*

Name ______________________________

I see the  station.

I see the  bus.

I see the  bus driver.

I see the  wheels.

High-Frequency Word: ***see***
Say and trace the word in each sentence. Read the sentence.

Name ____________________

I see Sam  .

swim

I See Sam

I see Sam  .

slide

I see Sam swing.

I see Sam  .

skate

Name ______________________________

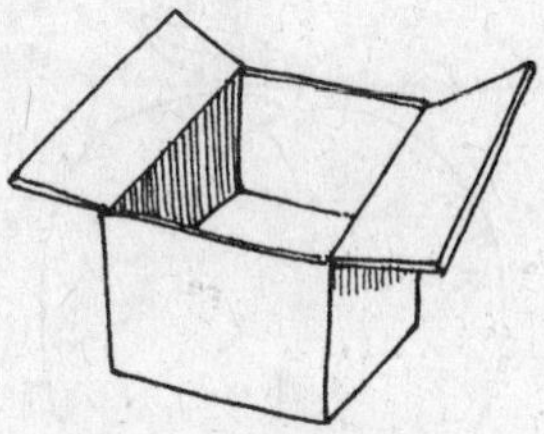

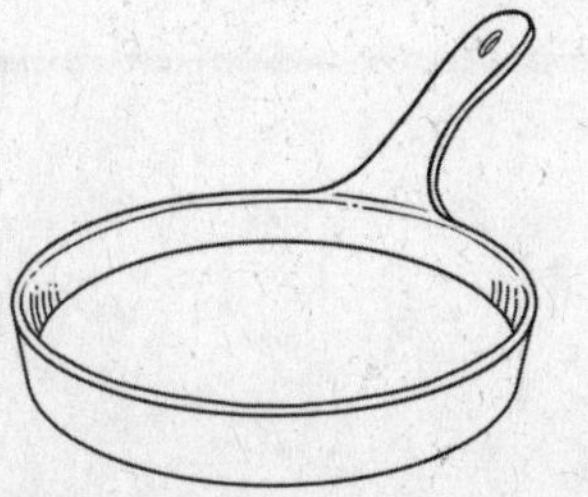

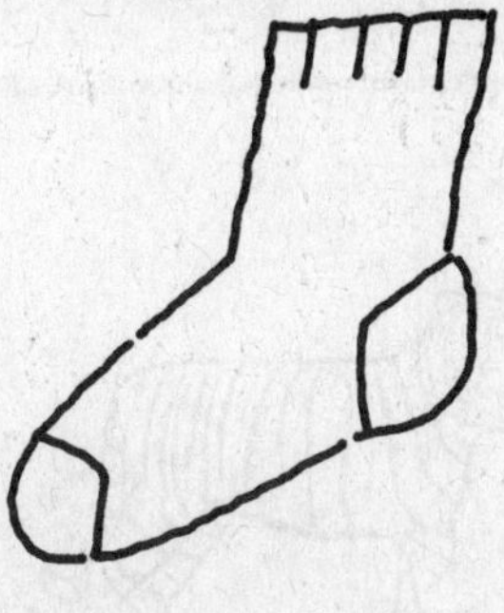

Phonemic Awareness: Phoneme Categorization

Listen to the beginning sound as I say each picture name: *pig, hen, hat.* Two words have the same sound at the beginning. Which word does not belong? Put an X on the picture whose name does not belong. *pen, bag, box;* *key, cat, pin;* *pan, sun, sock.*

Name ____________________

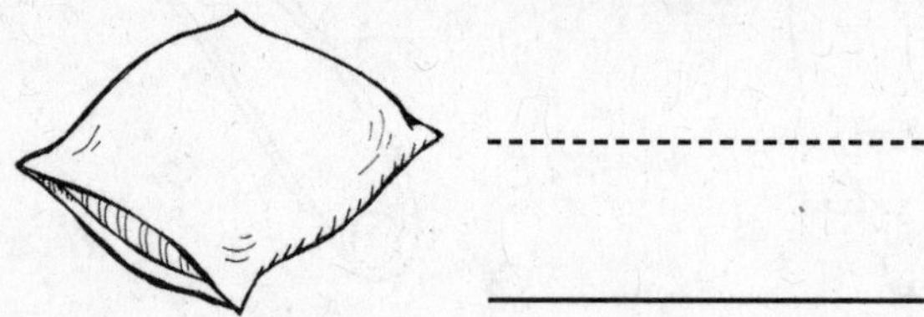

Phonics: initial *p*
Listen as I say each picture name. If the picture name begins with the /p/ sound, write *p* on the line. (*pail, peach, pillow, tiger*)

Name ____________________

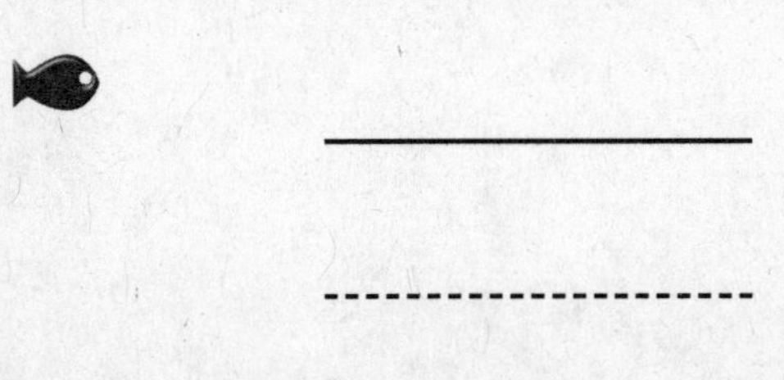

Phonics: initial, final *p*

Listen as I say each picture name. If you hear /p/ at the beginning of the word, write *p* on the first line. If you hear /p/ at the end of the word, write *p* on the last line. (*path, mop, sheep, pony*)

Name ______________________________

I am a  bear .

I am a  squirrel .

I am a  deer .

I am a  bird .

High-Frequency Word: *a*
Say and trace the word in each sentence. Read the sentence.

Name ______________________

I can see Pam eat.

I Can See

I see Pam the  cat.

I see a can.

I see a 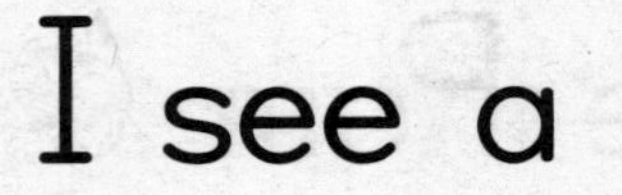 .

bowl

Name ____

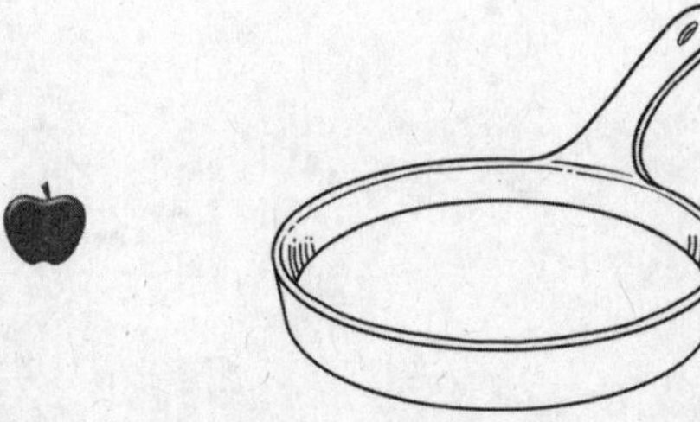

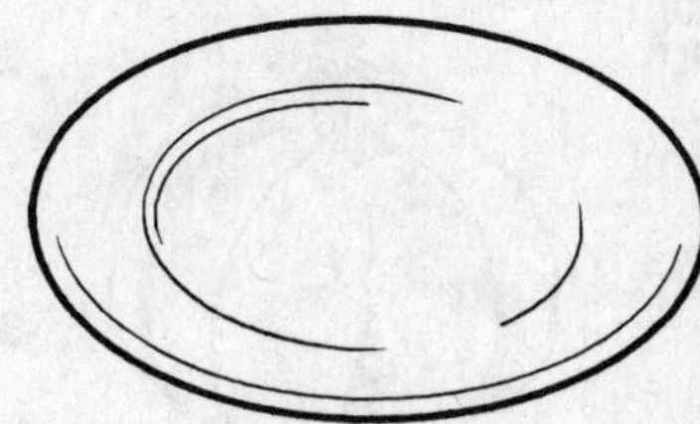

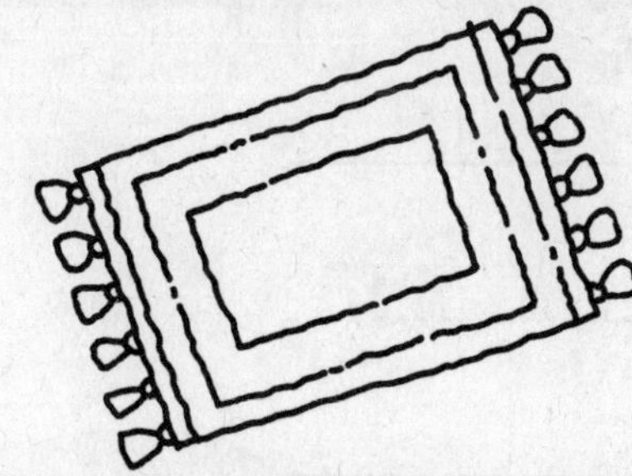

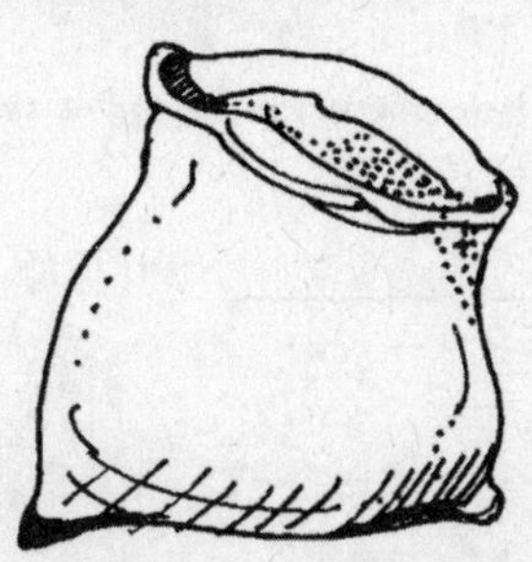

Phonemic Awareness: Phoneme Isolation
Listen to this word: *tell*. Listen for the beginning sound. /t/ /e/ /l/. Now listen to each picture name: *pan, wig, tack*. Circle the picture that has the same beginning sound as *tell*.
★ *nose* (*net, cab, dish*); *red* (*cat, rug, fin*); *tape* (*top, sack, bug*)

Name ____

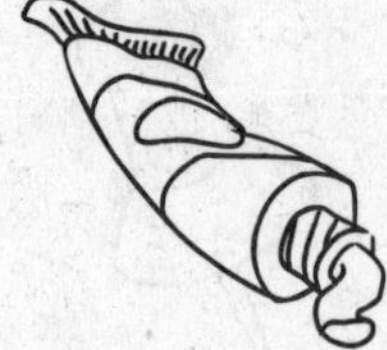

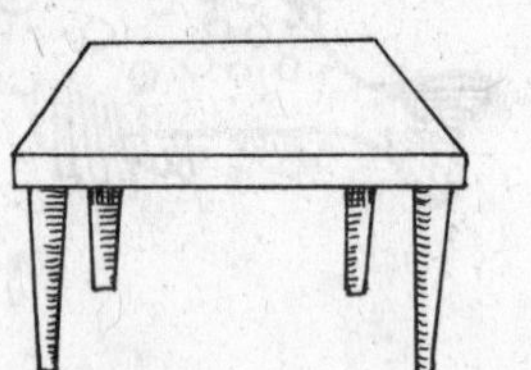

Phonics: initial *t*
Listen as I say each picture name. If the picture name begins with the /t/ sound, write *t* on the line. (*tube, pumpkin, table, towel*)

Name ______________________________

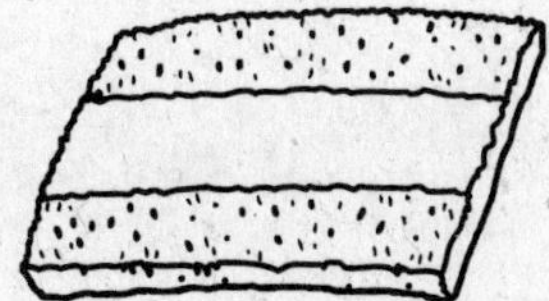

ma

sa

ap

pa

Phonics: initial, final *t*
Listen as I say each picture name. Trace the letters. Then write the missing letter *t*. (*mat, sat, tap, pat*)

Name ______________________________

like

I like

I like

I like

High-Frequency Words: *like*

Say and trace the word *like.* Say and trace the word in each sentence. Read each sentence. Draw a picture in each box to show something you like.

Name ______________________

I like the rain.

I Like

I like the coat.

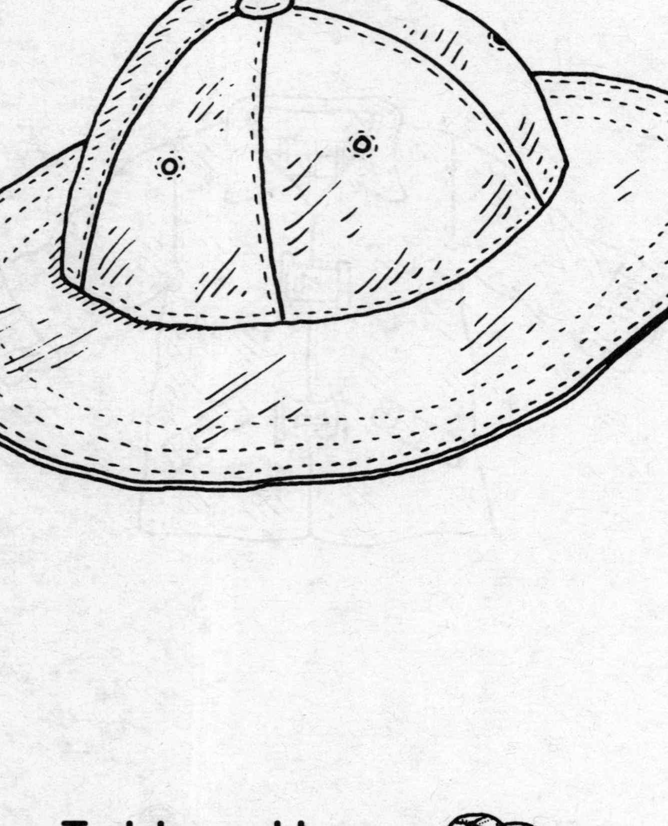

I like the hat.

I like the 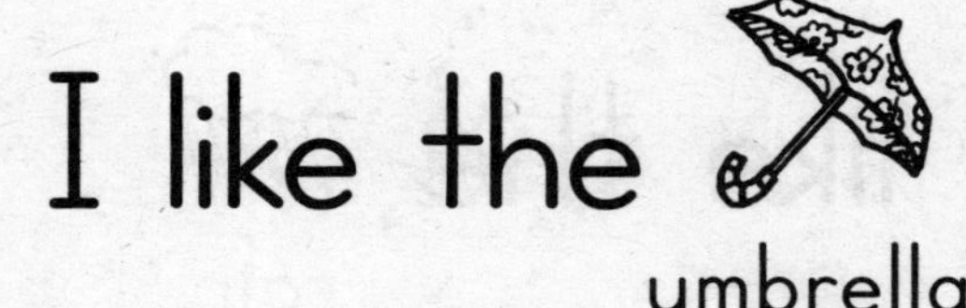 umbrella.

Name ______________________________

 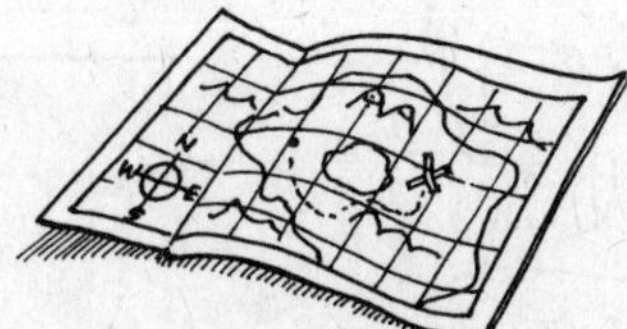  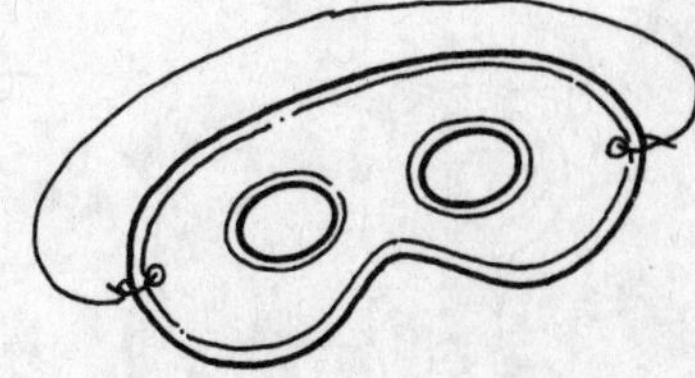

 2+1=3  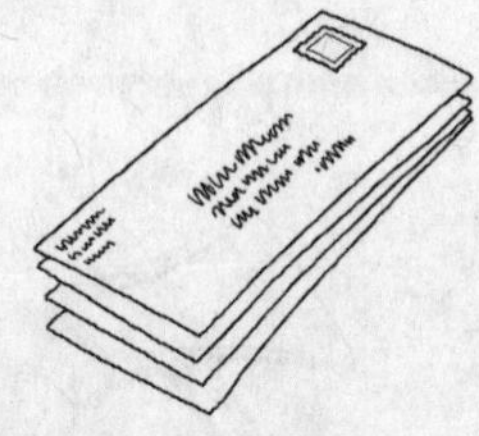

   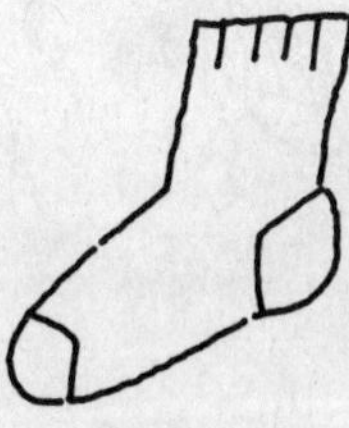

  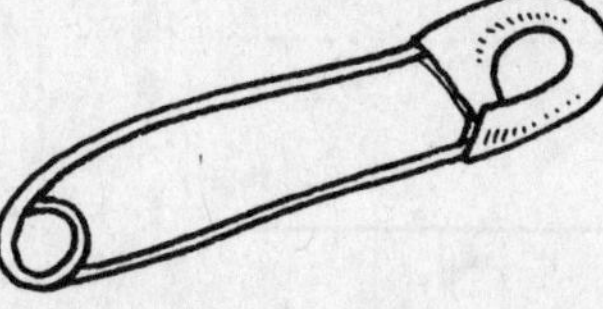 

Phonemic Awareness: Phoneme Blending

Listen as I say the sounds in a word. Blend the sounds to form a word. Then circle the picture that names the word. /m/ /a/ /p/; /m/ /a/ /th/; /s/ /o/ /k/; /p/ /i/ /n/; <sun> /b/ /ē/.

Name ______________________________

Phonics: Review: short *a, m, s, p, t*
Listen as I say each picture name. Write the letter that each picture name begins with.
(*pig, mix, ax, ten, pen, sock, six, top*)

Write

Name ____________________

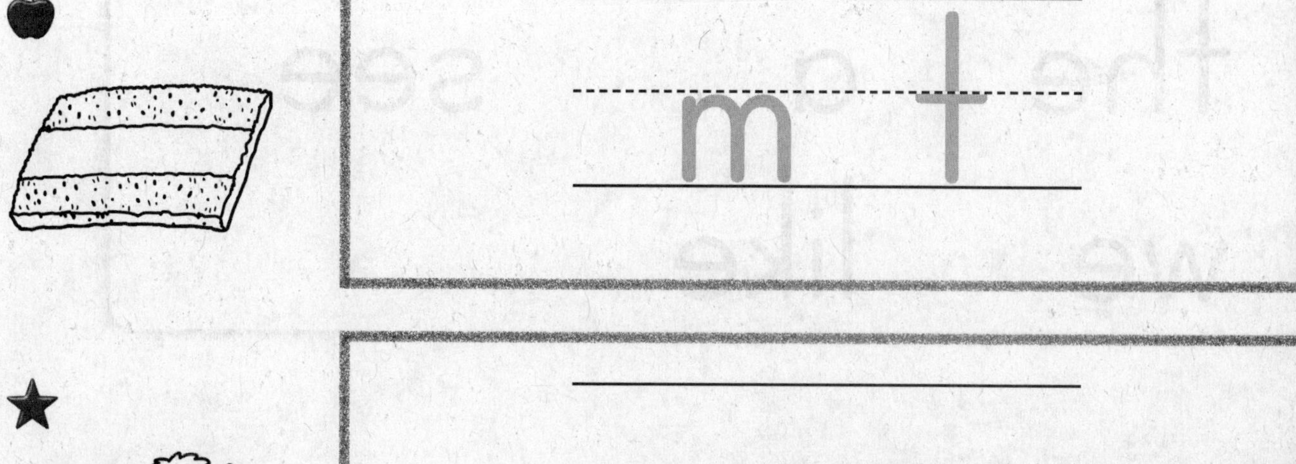

Phonics: Review short *a, m, s, p, t*
Listen as I say each picture name. Fill in the missing letter for each word. Then trace the word. (*mat, tap, map, sat*)

Name ______________________________

the a see
we like

We see a mat.

★

We like the mat.

We see a map.

High-Frequency Words: ***a, like, see, the, we***
Say the words. Read the words. Write the words. Read each sentence. Say and trace the words to finish the sentences.

Name ______________________

Pat can see the skates.

We Can See

Sam can see a  truck.

Sam can see the  .

trains

Sam can see the 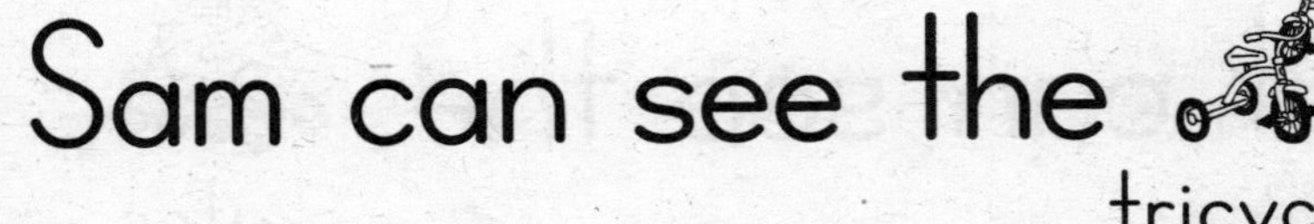 .

tricycles

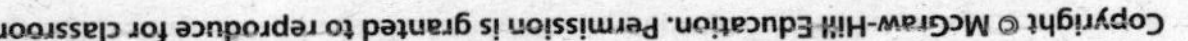

Name ____________________

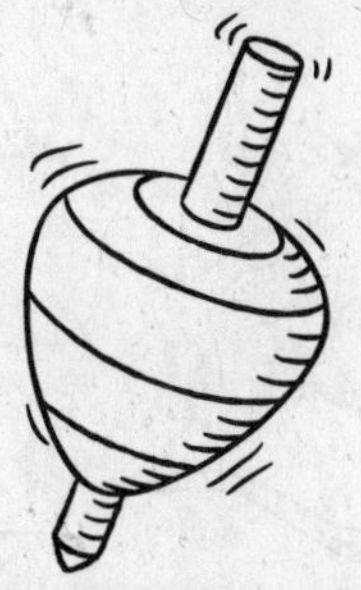

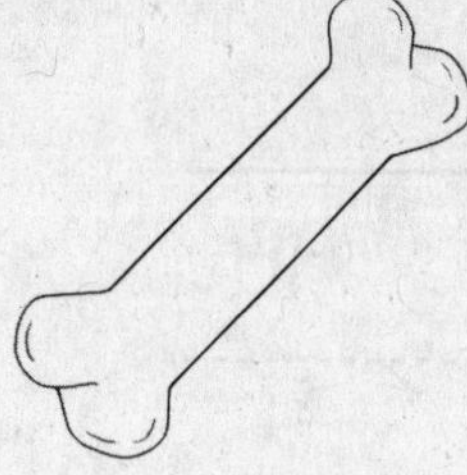
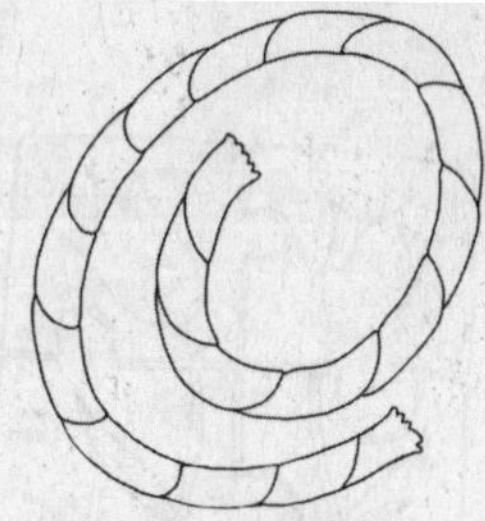

Phonemic Awareness: Phoneme Categorization
Listen as I say each picture name. (sun, bug, mop) Place an X over the word that does not have the same beginning sound. Repeat with the star row, the tree row, and the fish row (top, pig, rock; cat, bone, rope; fish, lid, boat).

Name ______________________________

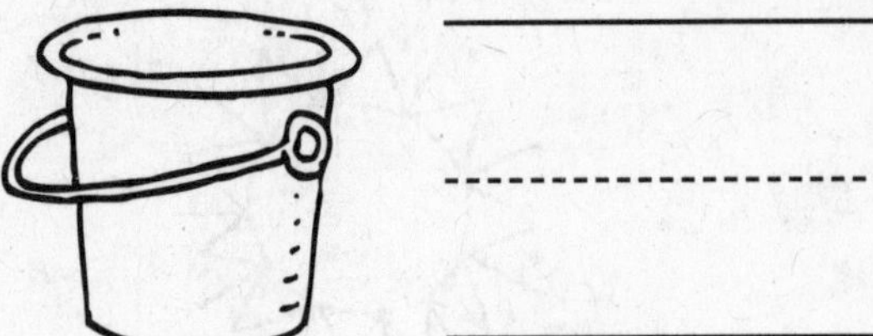

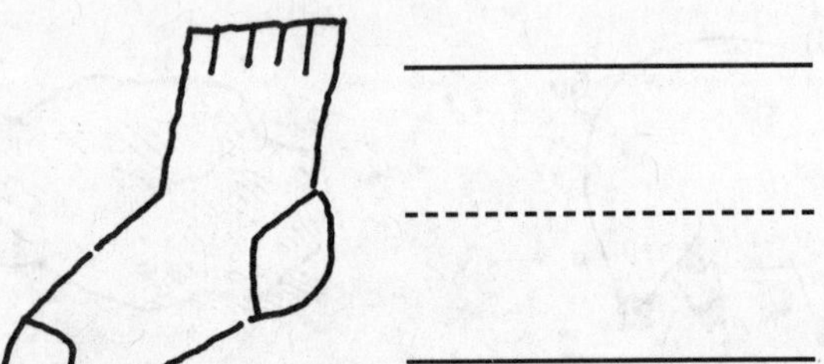

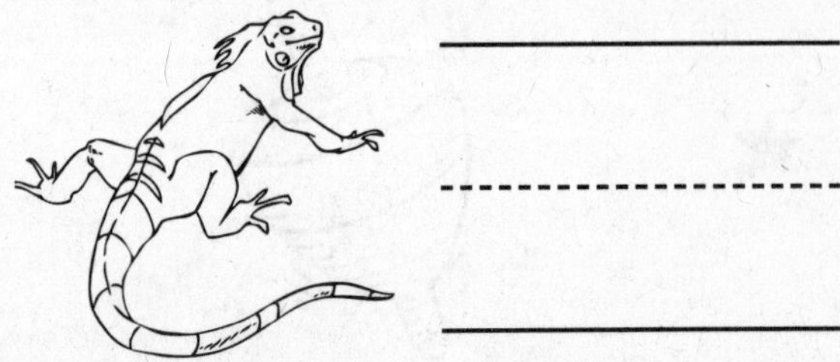

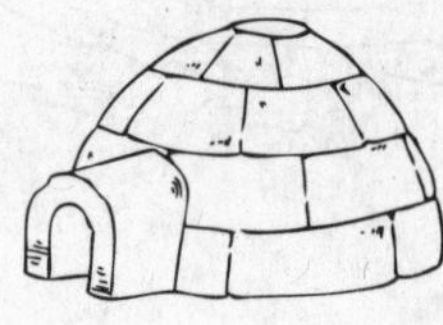

Phonics: Review Initial Letter-Sounds
Listen as I say each picture name. Say the picture name after me. Write the letter that begins each picture name on the line. (moon, pail, sock, iguana, puzzle, mouse, igloo, sun.)

Name ____________________

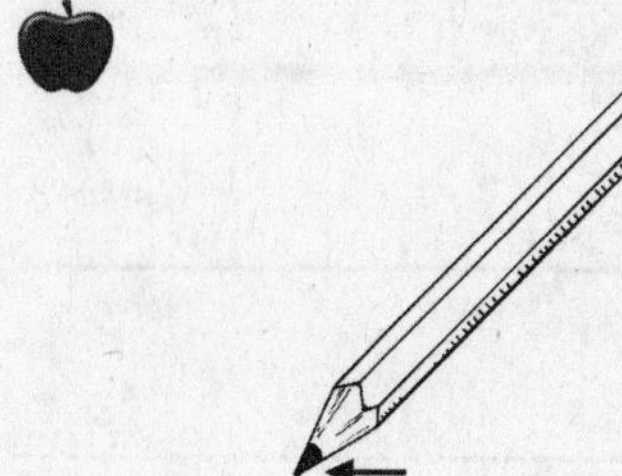

tip

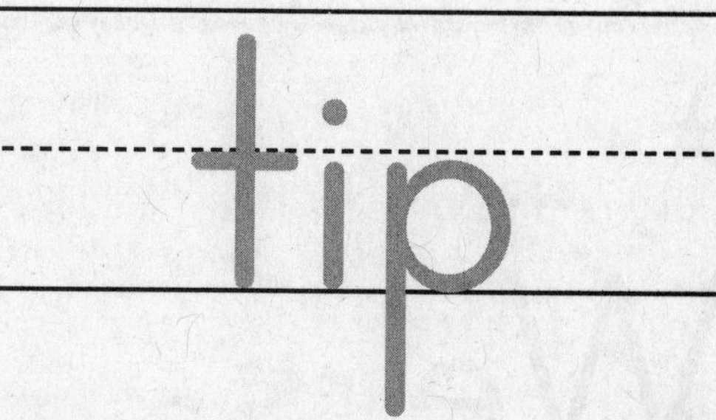

sip

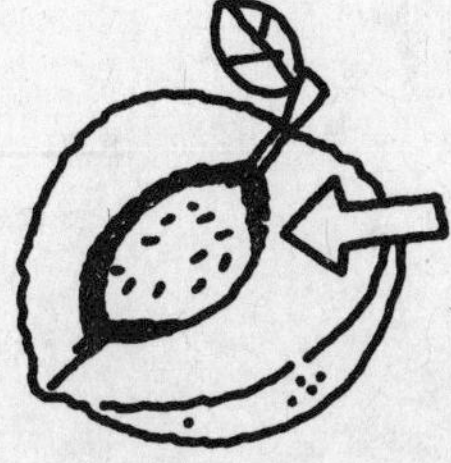

pit

Phonics: Blend and Build
Listen as I say each word. Trace each letter in the word. Blend the sounds and read each word. Then write the word on the line. (tip, sip, pit.)

Name ____________________

We like . like

We see .

See the .

We see a .

High-Frequency Words
Say the picture name and read each sentence. Trace the word in grey. Write the word on the line.

Name ______________________________

We like to  !

play

We Like

We like to  .

play

We like to    .

jump

We like to  .

run

Name ________________________________

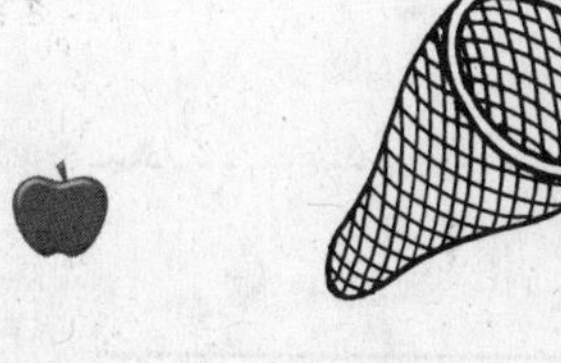
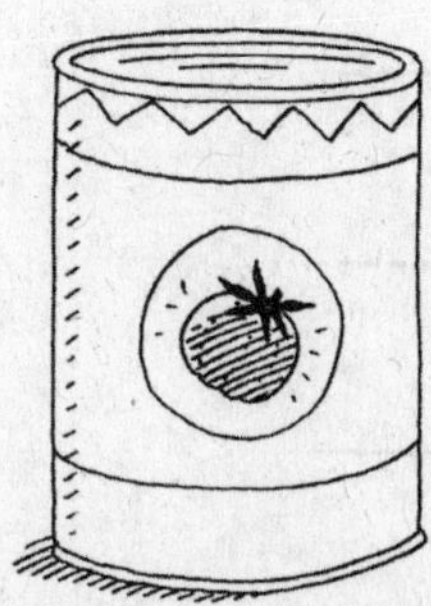

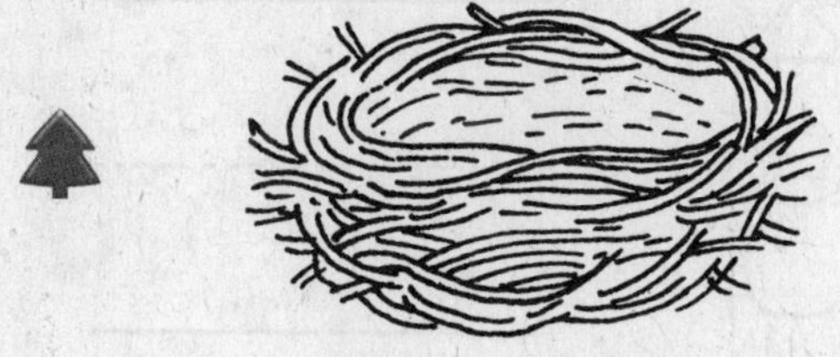

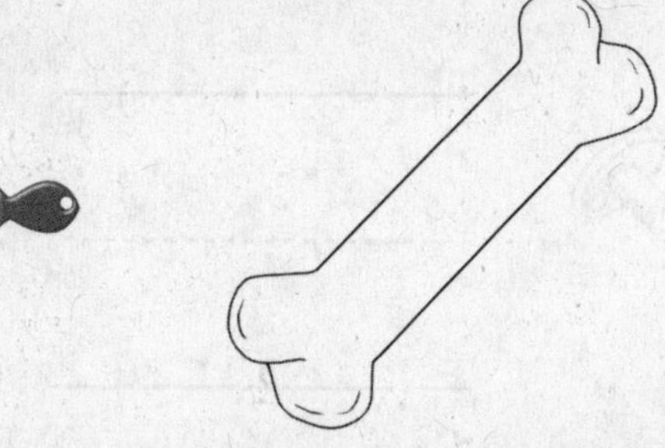

Phonemic Awareness: Phoneme Isolation
Listen as I say each word. if the first sound in the word is /n/, draw a circle around the picture. If the last sound in the word is /n/, draw a square around the picture.
net, can, nose; fan, sun, knot; nest, hen, night; bone, nail, nine.

Name ________________________________

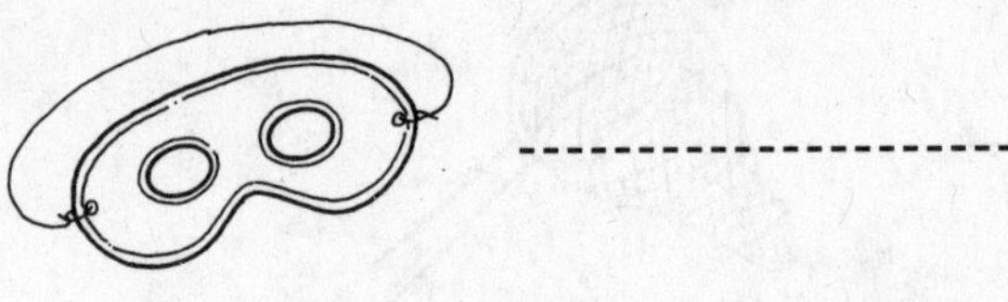

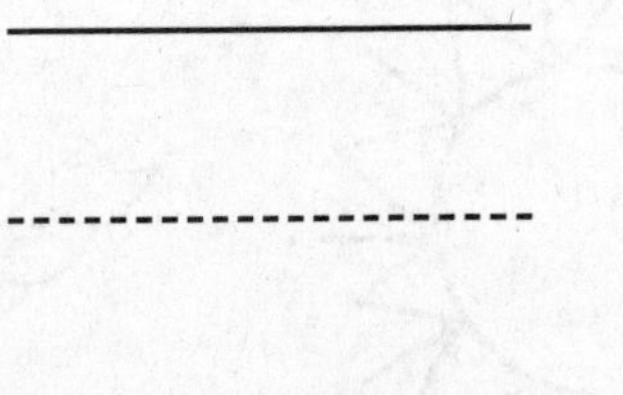

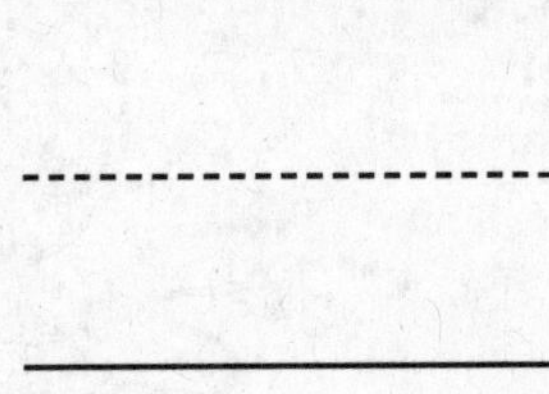

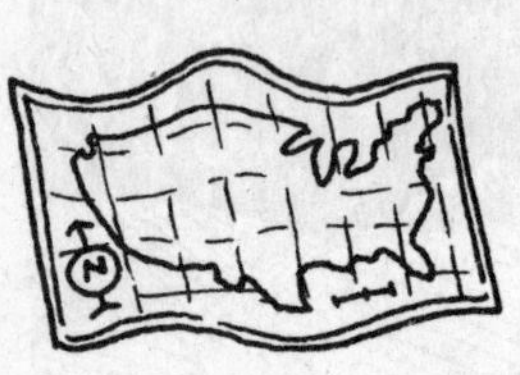

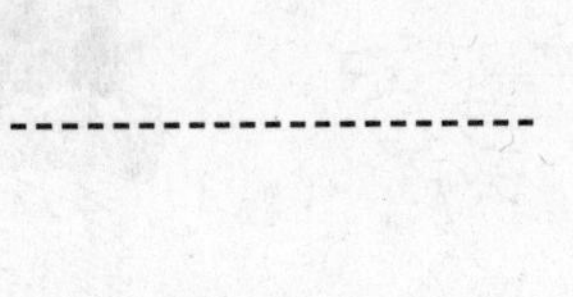

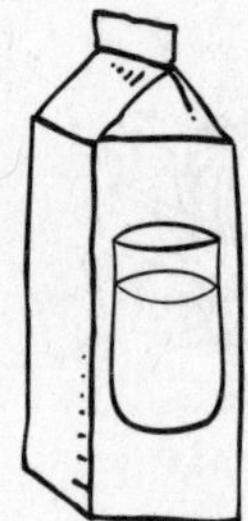

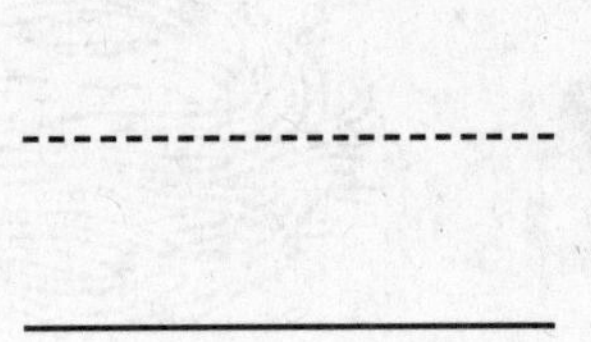

Phonics: initial *n, m*
Listen as I say the picture name. If the name begins with the /n/ sound, write the letter *n* on the line. If the name begins with the /m/ sound, write the letter *m* on the line. *(nest, mask, nut, nine, map, milk, nose, nail)*

Name ____________________

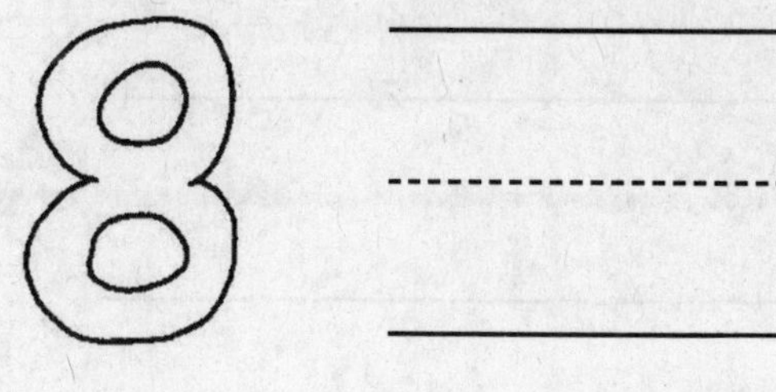

Phonics: final *n, t*

Listen as I say the picture name. If the name ends with the /n/ sound, write the letter *n* on the line. If the name ends with the /t/ sound, write the letter *t* on the line. *(ten, moon, kite, fan, sun, eight, cat, pen)*

Name ________________________________

and

to

like

a

see

High-Frequency Words: ***a, and, like, see, to***
Say the word *and*. Then trace the word *and*. Write the word on the line. Repeat with the words *to, like, a, see.*

Name ______________________________

Nat and Nan pin it!

Nat and Nan

Can Nat and Nan  ?

paint

Nat and Nan paint.

Nat and Nan like it.

Name ____

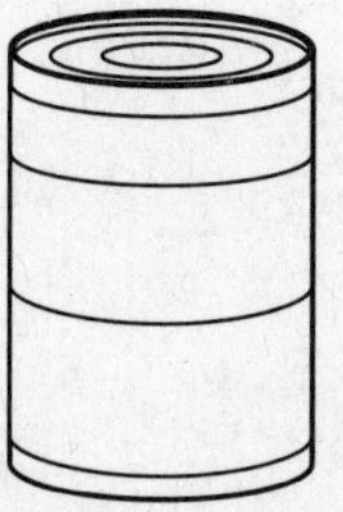

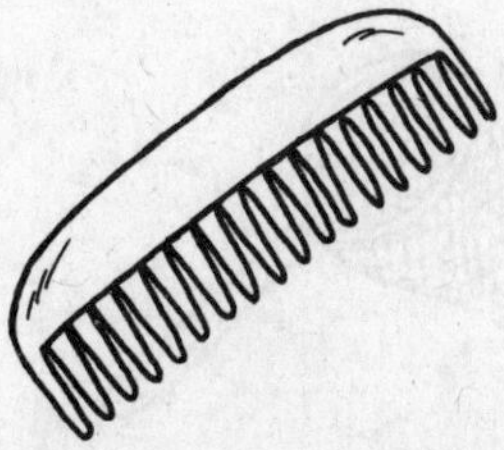

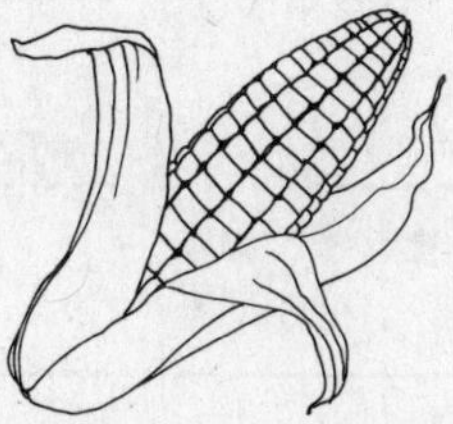

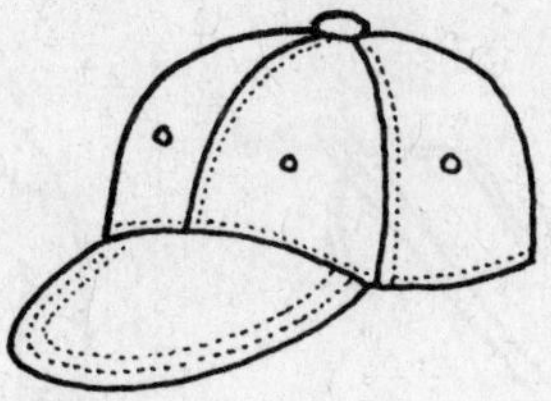

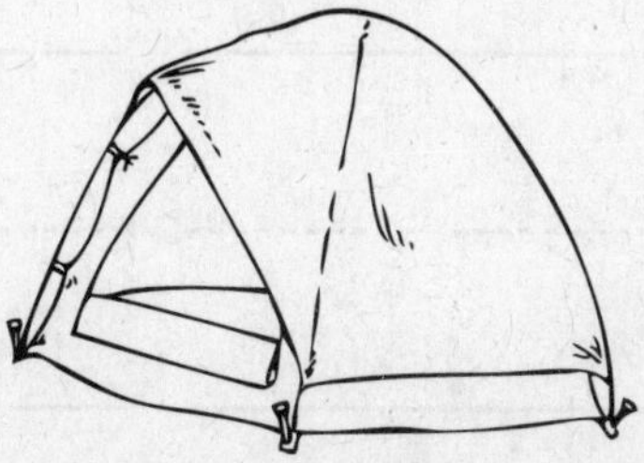

Phonemic Awareness: Phoneme Isolation
Listen as I say each picture name. Listen to the sounds at the beginning of each word. Circle the pictures whose names have the /k/ sound at the beginning. *(mop, can, comb)* Repeat with the star row, the tree row, and the fish row *(corn, pig, cat; cap, cake, nurse; car, cow, tent).*

Write

Name ___

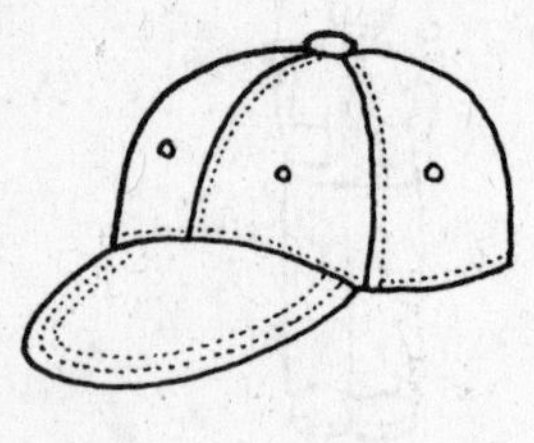

Phonics: initial /k/c
Listen as I say each picture name. Circle the picture whose name begins with the sound /k/. Write a *c* on the line below the picture. (net, corn; cup, nest; cap, nose; needle, coat)

Name ____

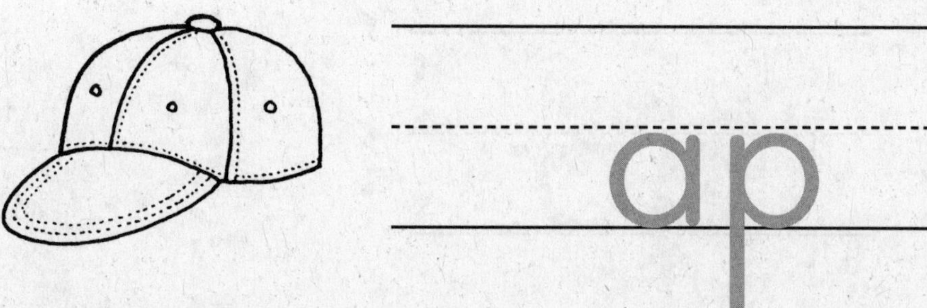

an

at

Phonics: initial *c*
Listen as I say each picture name. Fill in the missing letter for each word. Then trace the whole word and read the word. (cap, can, cat)

Name ______________________________

I can go .

A  can ________ .

A  can ________ .

A  can ________ .

High-Frequency Word: ***go***
Read the first sentence. Say the word *go*. Trace the word *go*. Then read the other sentences. Complete each sentence with the word *go*.

Name ______________________

Cam can go.

Cam in a Cap

See Cam in a tan cap.

Cam can  !

catch

Sam can 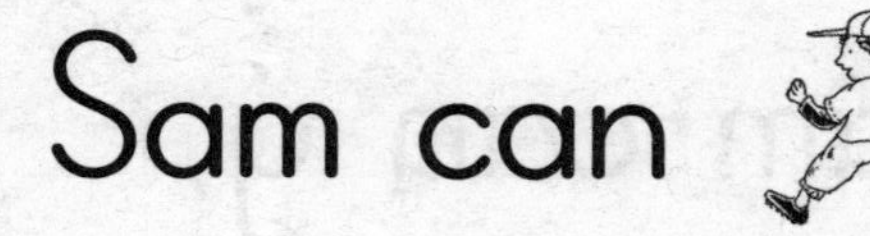 .

run

Name ___________________________

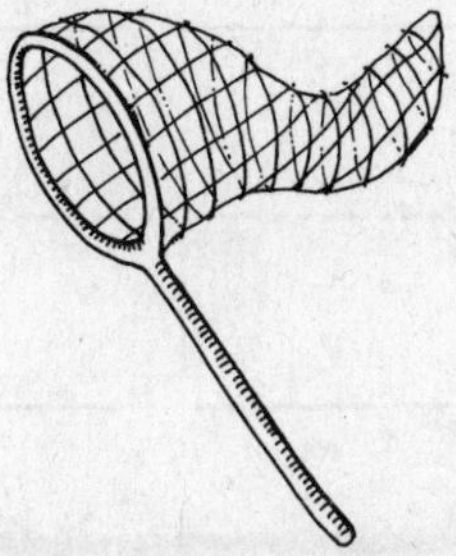

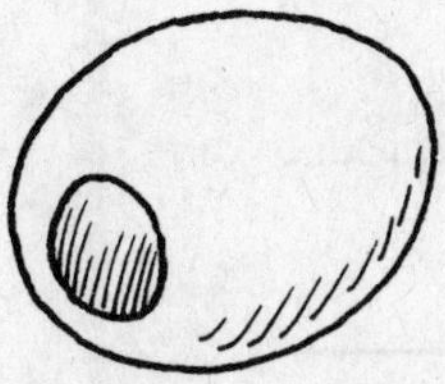

Phonemic Awareness: Phoneme Isolation
Listen as I say each picture name. *(octopus, can, duck)* Circle the picture in each row that begins with /o/. *(net, olive, cat; nut, seal, ox; cow, otter, tent)*

Name ______________________________

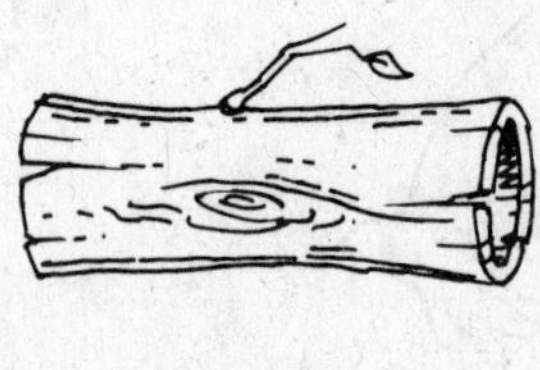

Phonics: short *o*

Listen as I say each picture name. Circle the picture whose name has the sound /o/ at the beginning. Write an *o* on the line below the picture. (octopus, apple, ant, ostrich) Listen as I say each picture name. Circle the picture whose name has the /o/ sound in the middle. Write an *o* on the line below the picture. (cat, log, rock, pan)

Name ______________________________

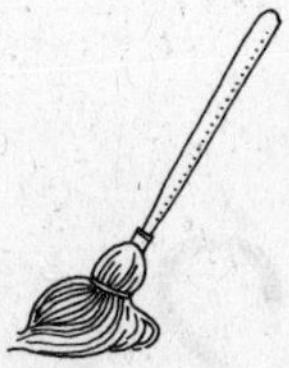

m p

t p

p t

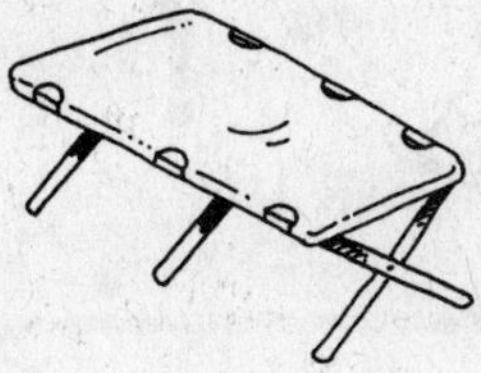

c t

M m

Phonics: short *o*
Listen as I say each picture name. Fill in the missing letters for each word. Then trace the whole word and read the word. (mop, top, pot, cot, Mom)

Name ______________________________

Can you tap?

Can ______  ?

Can ______  ?

Can ______  ?

High-Frequency Word: ***you***
Read the first sentence. Say and trace the word *you*. Complete each sentence with the word *you*. Then read the other sentences.

Name ______________________

You can pop it!

Can You Pin It On?

Tam can not pin it on.

Tom can not pin it on.

Pam can not pin it on.

Name ___________________________________

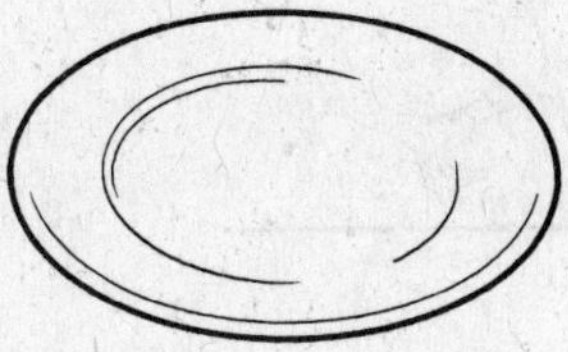

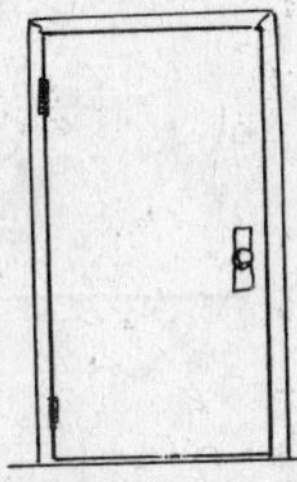

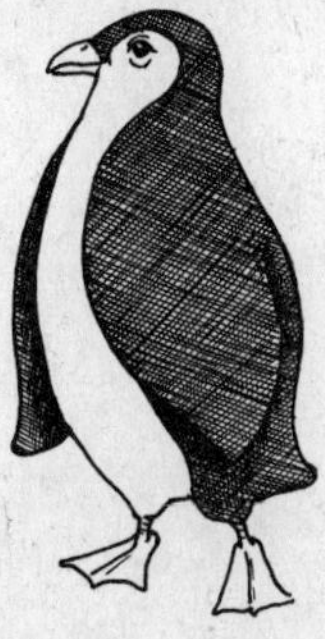

Phonemic Awareness: Phoneme Isolation
Listen as I say the picture names in the first row *(dog, duck, mouse).* Circle the pictures whose names begin with the same sounds. Repeat with the star row *(dish: pig, door),* the tree row *(desk, deer, horse),* and the fish row *(dance, penguin, dinosaur).*

Name ______________________________

Phonics: initial *d, o, t*

Listen as I say each picture name. If the name begins with the /d/ sound, write *d* on the line. If the name begins with the /o/ sound, write *o* on the line. If the name begins with the /t/ sound, write *t* on the line. *(dime, dig, otter, duck, deer, tooth, tent, desk)*

Name ____________________

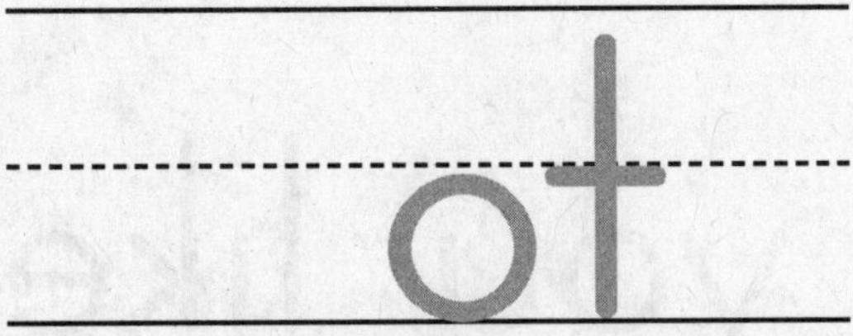

ot

a

ma

pa

Phonics: *d*
Listen as I say each picture name. Fill in the missing letter for each word. Then trace the word. (dot, dad, mad, pad)

Name ______________________________

Do you like 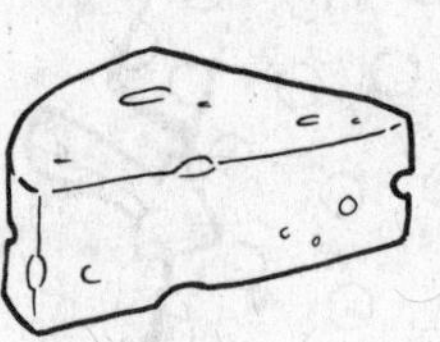 ?

______ you like 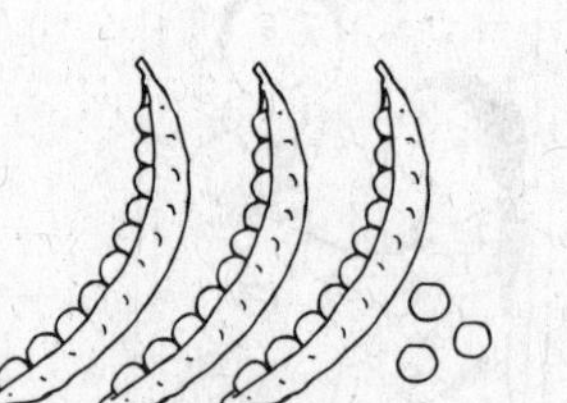 ?

______ you see a  ?

______ you see a  ?

High-Frequency Word: ***do***
Read the first sentence. Say and trace the word *Do*. With a partner, read the other sentences. Complete each sentence with the word *Do*. Remember to use a capital *D* at the beginning of a sentence.

Name ____________________

"Sit, Don and Dan."

Sid, Don, and Dan

Don and Dan do it.

Sid sees sad Dan.

Sid  sees mad Don.

Name ______________________________

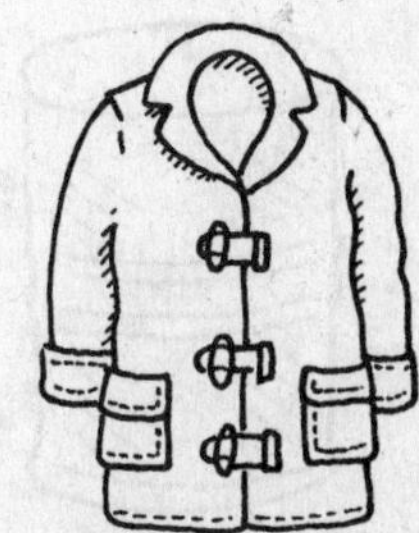

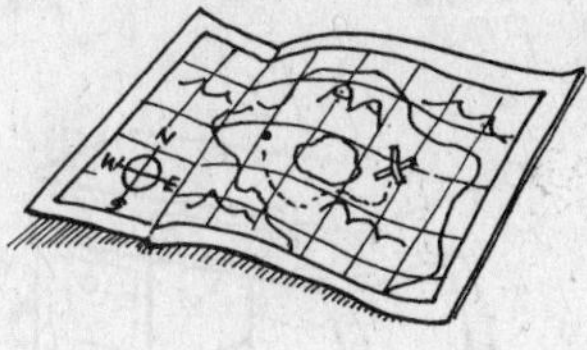

Phonemic Awareness: Phoneme Identity

Listen carefully as I say each picture name. 🍎 Circle the pictures in the row that have the sound /k/ as in *cap.* (*cat, ten, coat*) ★ Circle the pictures in the row that have the sound /d/ as in *dime.* (*tent, deer, dog*) 🌲 Circle the pictures in the row that have the sound /n/ as in *nap.* (*nine, nest, map*) 🐟 Circle the pictures in the row that have the sound /o/ as in *ox.* (*apple, octopus, ox*).

Write

Name ______________________________

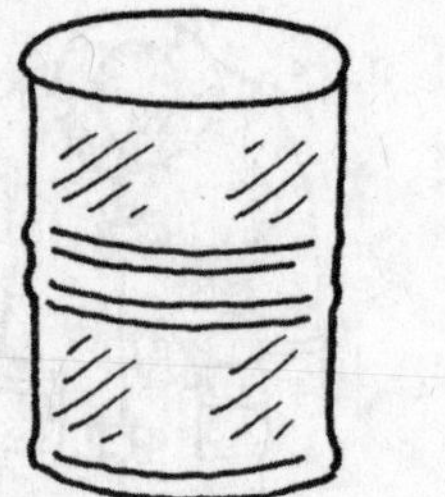

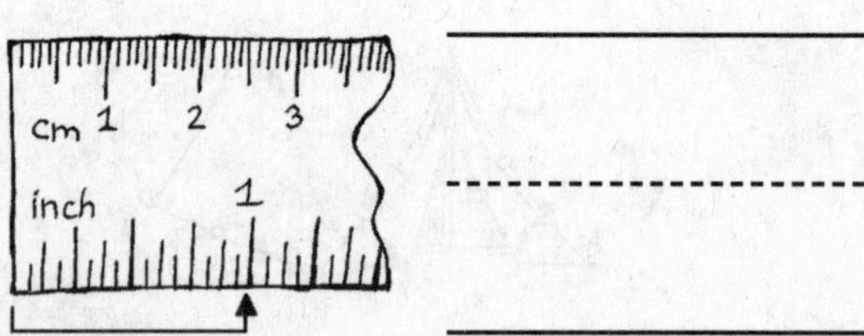

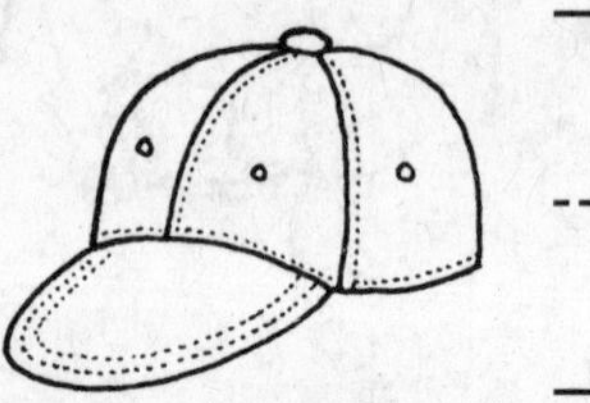

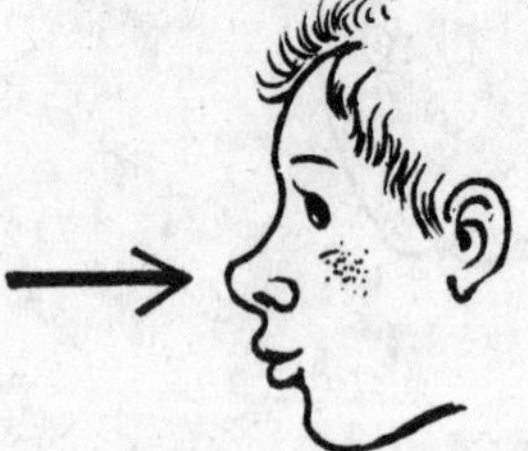

Phonics: Review short *i*, short *o*, *n*, *c*, *d*
Listen as I say each picture name. Write the letter that stands for the sound each picture name begins with. (*can, nut, dog, inch, desk, ox, cap, nose*)

Name ______________________________

can dot nap pin

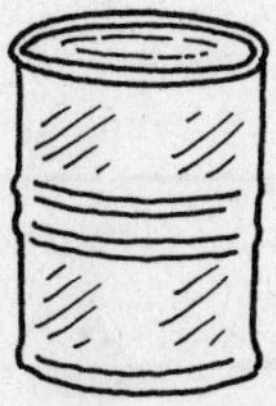

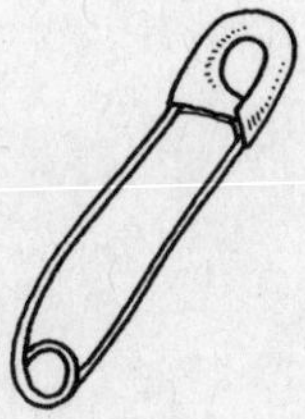

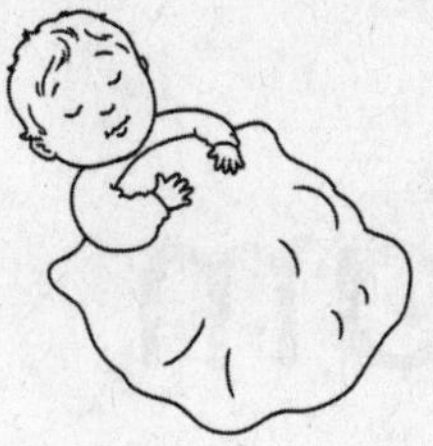

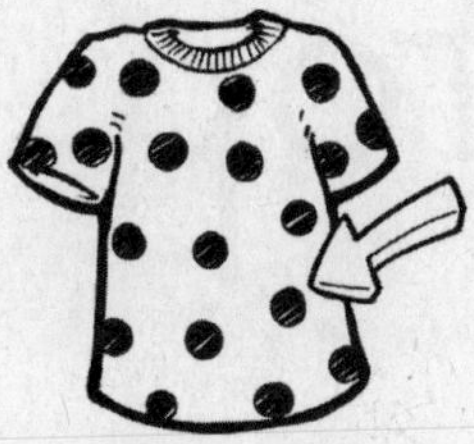

Phonics: short *i*, short *o, n, c, d*
Listen as I say each picture name. Write a word from the box to name each picture.
(*can, pin, nap, dot*)

Name ______________________________

and do go to you

🍎 Do you go to the top?

★ Nan ________ Cam ________ ________ the top.

High-Frequency Words: ***and, do, go, to, you***
Say each word in the box. Spell each word aloud. Trace the word with your pencil.
🍎 Trace the words to complete the sentence. Read the sentence. ★ Complete the sentence.
Write *and* in the first blank, *go* in the second, and *to* in the third. Read the sentence.

Name ______________________

Cat can throw to Dad.

Cat can do it!

Dad!

Tom can look like Dad.

Tom, you can do it!

Dad can go on a bike.

Sid can do it!

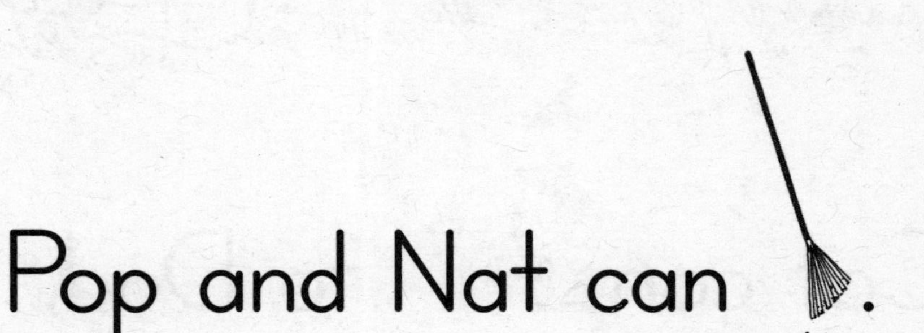

Pop and Nat can rake.

Nat can do it!

Name ____

 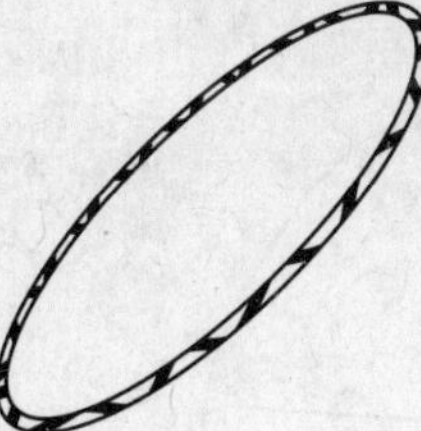 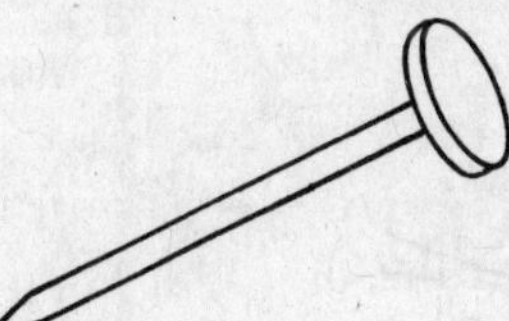 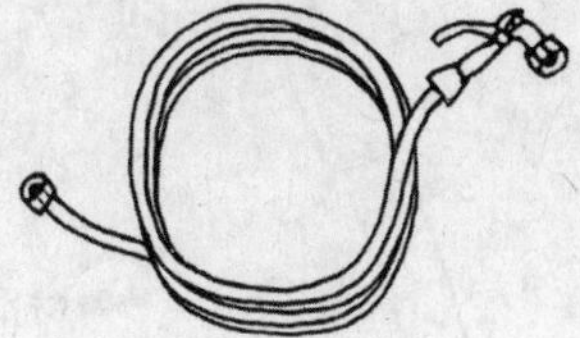

Phonemic Awareness: Phoneme Isolation
Listen carefully as I say each picture name. Circle the two pictures in each row that begin with /h/.
(ten, horse, house; hammer, otter, hummingbird; hoop, nail, hose; hog, hen, duck)

Write

Name ____________________

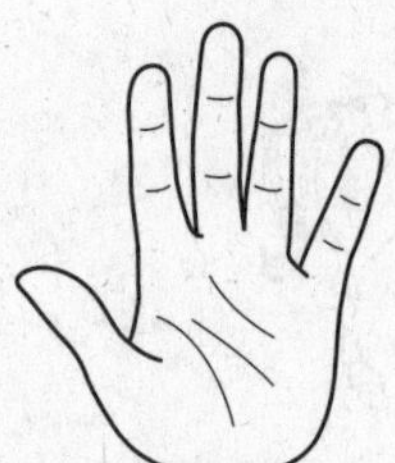

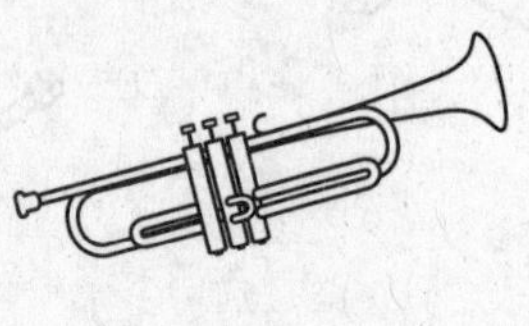

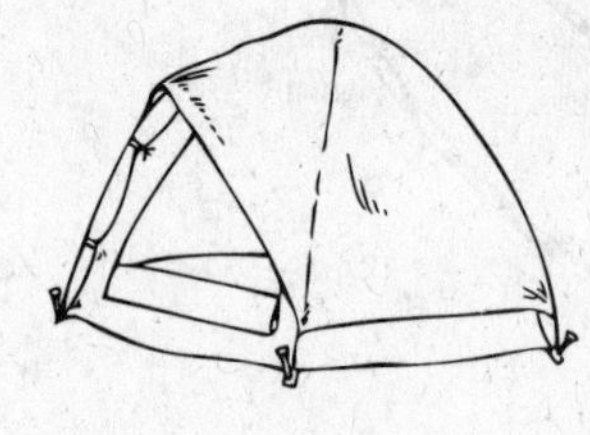

Phonics: initial *h*
Listen as I say each picture name. Circle the picture whose name has the sound /h/ at the beginning. Write an *h* on the line below the picture. *(cow, hand; heart, ant; pen, horn; tent, horse)*

Name ____

at

ot

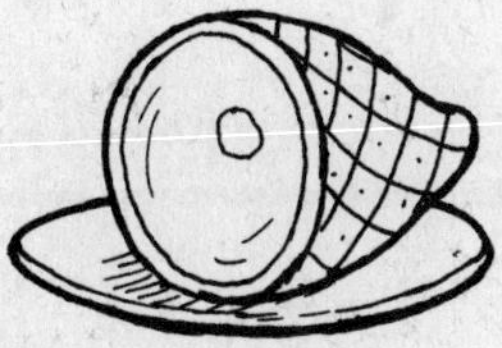

am

ip

op

Phonics: initial *h*
Listen as I say each picture name. Fill in the missing letter for each word. Then trace the word.
(hat, hot, ham, hip, hop)

Name ______________________________

🍎

I like ___my___ hat.

★

I see ______  .

dog

🌲

______ cat can  .

jump

I can hop to ______  .

mom

High-Frequency Word: ***my***

Read the first sentence. Say and trace the word *my*. With a partner, read the other sentences. Complete each sentence with the word *my*. Remember to use a capital *M* at the beginning of a sentence.

Name ____________________

"My dad has [water]."

I am not hot!"

Hot!

Cam can not hop.

"I am hot!"

Cam can not mop.

"I am hot!"

Cam can not hit.

"I am hot!"

Circle

Name ______________________________

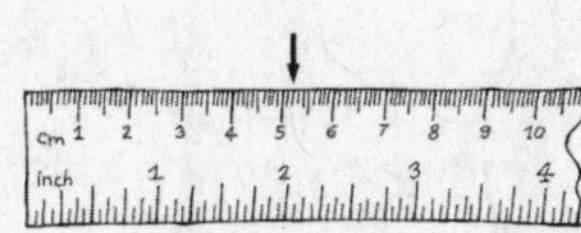

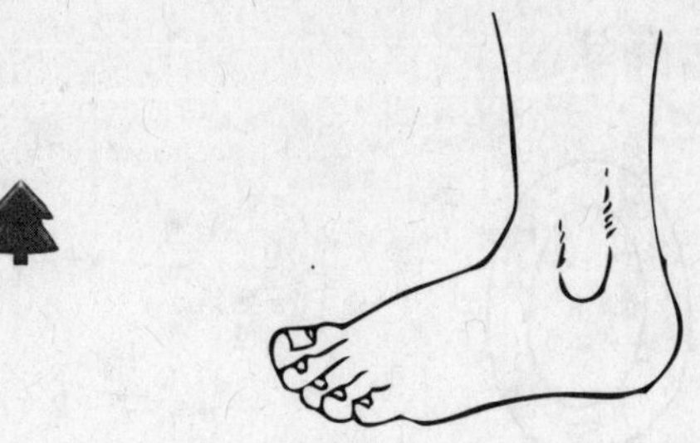

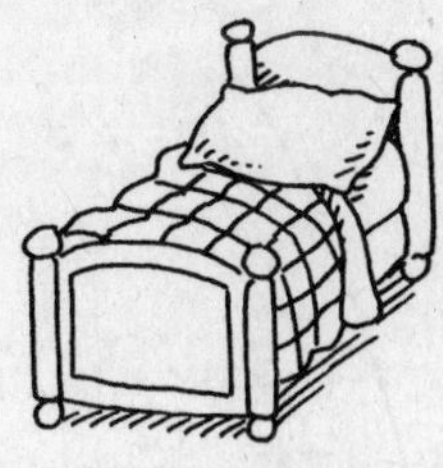

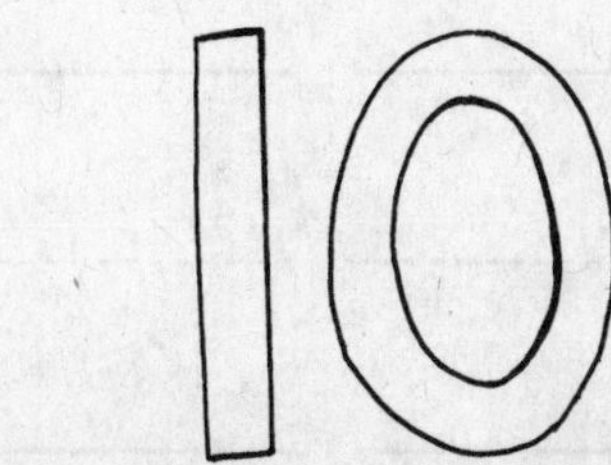

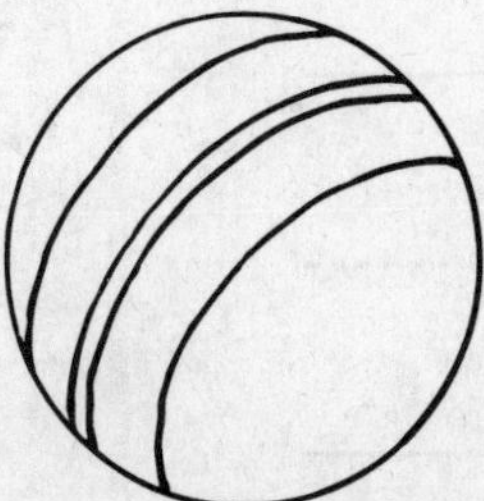

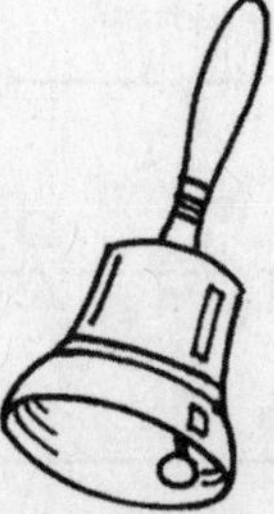

Phonemic Awareness: Phoneme Isolation

Listen as I say each picture name. Circle the two pictures in each row that begin with /e/. *(egg, inch, elephant; alligator, elevator, elbow.)* Listen as I say each picture name. Circle the two pictures in each row that have /e/ in the middle. *(foot, leg, bed; ten, ball, bell.)*

Name ______________________________

Phonics: short *e*

Listen as I say each picture name. Circle the picture whose name has the sound /e/ at the beginning. Write an *e* on the line below the picture. (elephant, cat; bib, egg) Listen as I say each picture name. Circle the picture whose name has the /e/ sound in the middle. Write an *e* on the line below the picture. (pen, log; ten, dog)

Write

Name ___

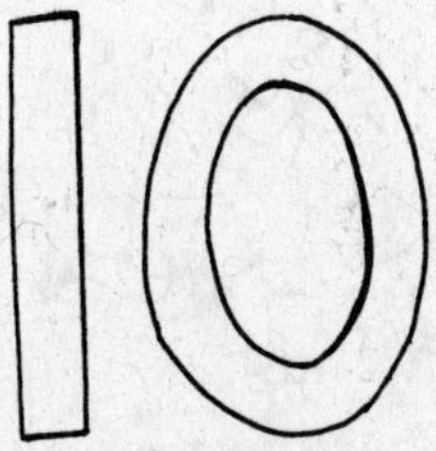

t n

n t

h n

m n

p n

Phonics: short *e*
Listen as I say each picture name. Fill in the missing letter. Read each word. Then trace the word.
(ten, net, hen, men, pen)

Name ______________________________

🍎

The men are ______  .

running

★

You ______ my  .

friend

______ you Ted?

We ______  .

twins

High-Frequency Word: ***are***
Read the first sentence. Say and trace the word *are*. Then read the other sentences with a partner. Complete each sentence with the word *are*. Remember to use a capital *A* at the beginning of a sentence.

Name ____________________

Ten [chicks] can go.

Ed can pet a [chick].

Hen in a Pen

Ed had a pet hen.

Pet hen Nan can go.

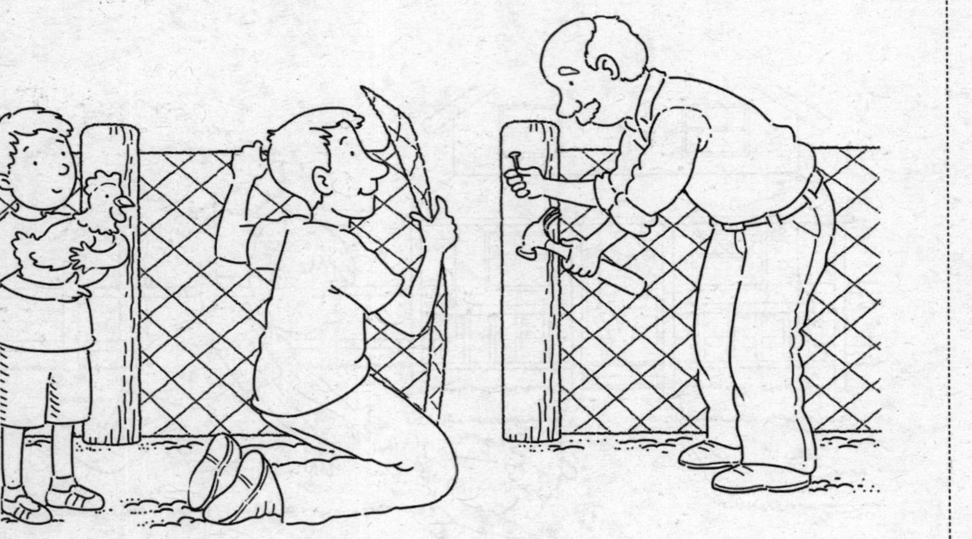

Men can tap, tap, tap.

Nan can not go.

Pet hen Nan had ten.

Ten eggs are in the pen.

Name ___________________________________

I.

2.

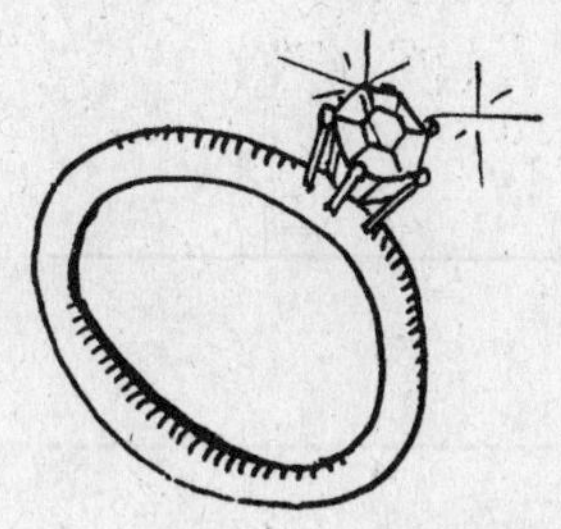
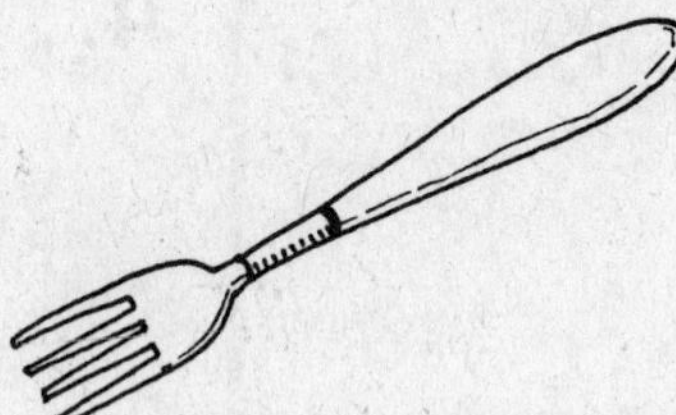

3.

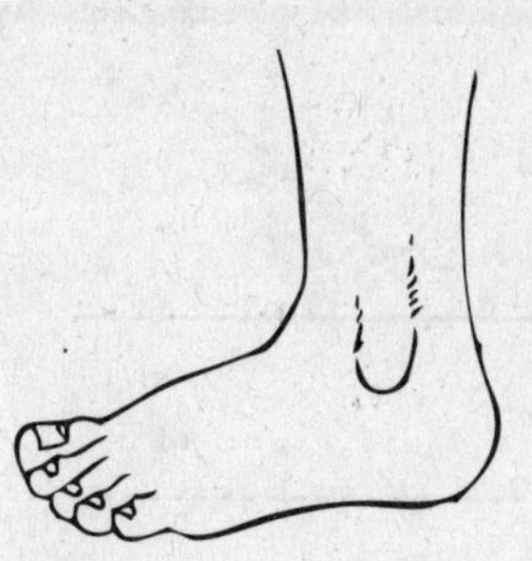

4.

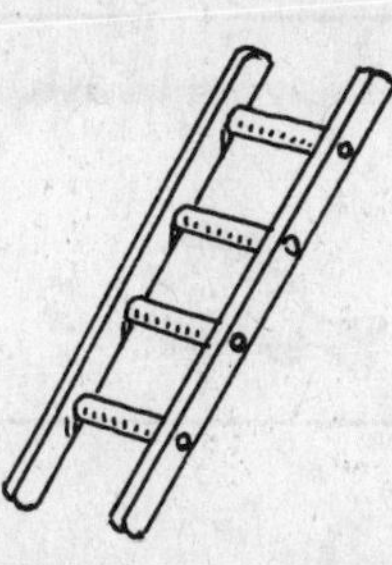
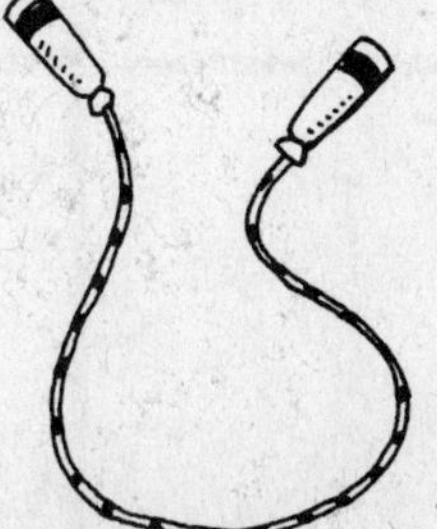

Phonemic Awareness: **Phoneme Isolation**
Listen as I say each picture name. I-2: Circle the pictures that begin with /f/. *(rake, house, fan; ring, fork, nest)* 3-4: Circle the pictures that begin with /r/. *(foot, seal, rose; ladder, rope, five)*

Name ____________________

1. 

2. 

3. 

4. 

5. 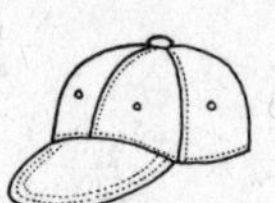

6. 

7. 

8. 

Phonics: **initial *f*, initial *r***
Listen as I say each picture name. If the picture name begins with the sound /f/, write an *f* on the line below the picture. If the picture name begins with /r/, write an *r* on the line below the picture.
(rose, fox, sun, four, hat, rake, ring, fish)

Name ____________________

1. 

an

2. 

in

3. 

am

4. 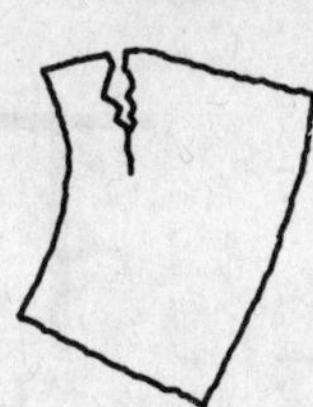

ip

5. 

at

Phonics: **initial *f*, initial *r***
Listen as I say each picture name. Fill in the missing letter for the beginning of each word. Then trace the word. *(fan, fin, ram, rip, rat)*

Name ______________________________

1.

He sat.

2.

______ ran with Sam.

3.

Ron ran 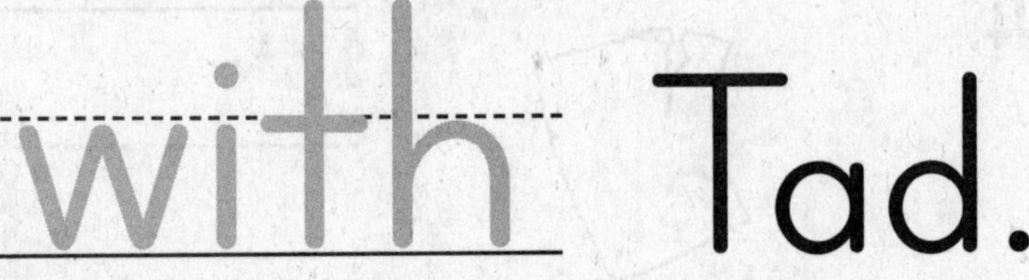

Tad.

4.

He sat ______ Tad.

High-Frequency Words: *he, with*

1. Read the sentence. Say and trace the word *He*. 2. Read the sentence. Complete the second sentence with the word *He*. 3. Read the sentence. Say and trace the word *with*. 4. Read the sentence. Complete the sentence with the word *with*.

Name ____________________

Rod ran to nap.

He can nap on Ron.

Rod Can

Can Rod see Tam?

Rod can rap-a-tap.

Rod sat with Tam.

Tam fed Rod ham.

Rod had to go.

He can not sit.

Name ____________________

1.

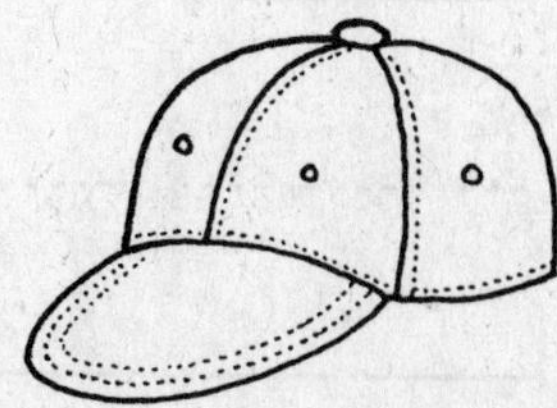

2.

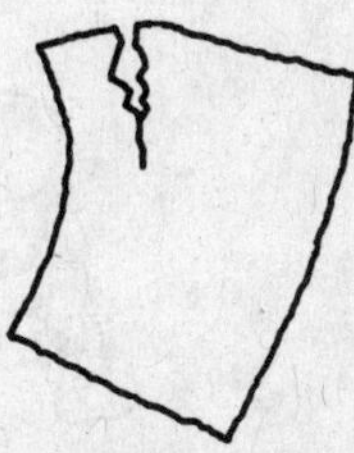
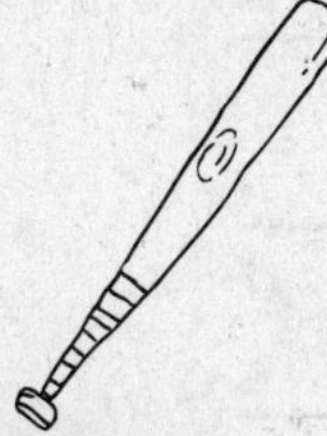

3.

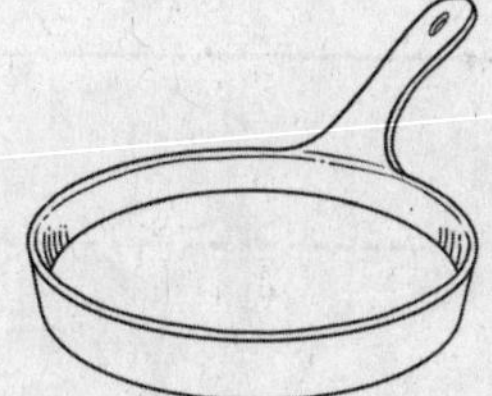

4.

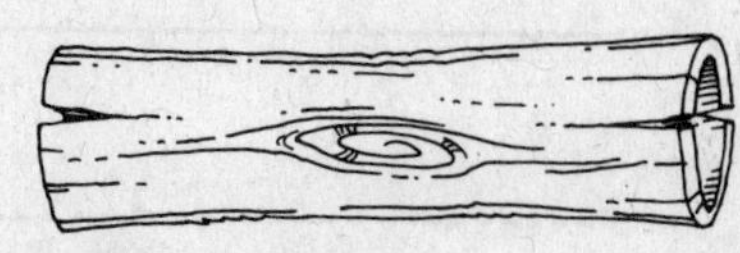

5.

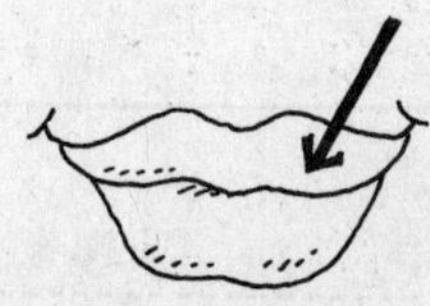

Phonemic Awareness: **Phoneme Isolation**
I will say a word; listen for the beginning sound. Then listen to the answer choices.
Circle the picture that has a name with the same beginning sound as the word I say.
1. lamp; leaf, nut, cap 2. bus; rip, bat, phone 3. bell; bee, dog, pan 4. lab; heart, sun, log
5. ball; can, bag, lip

Name ______________________________

1. 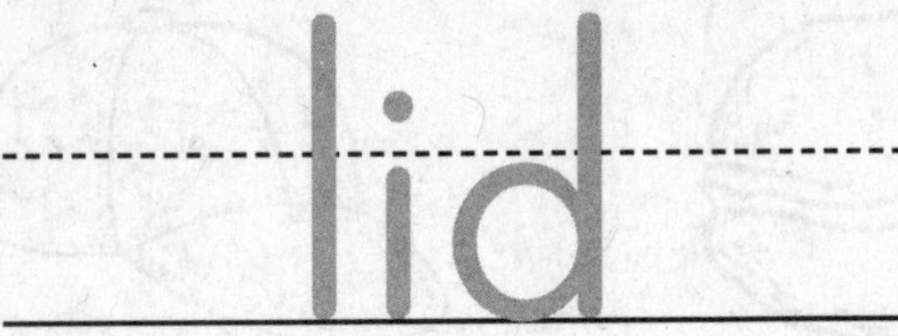

2. 

3. 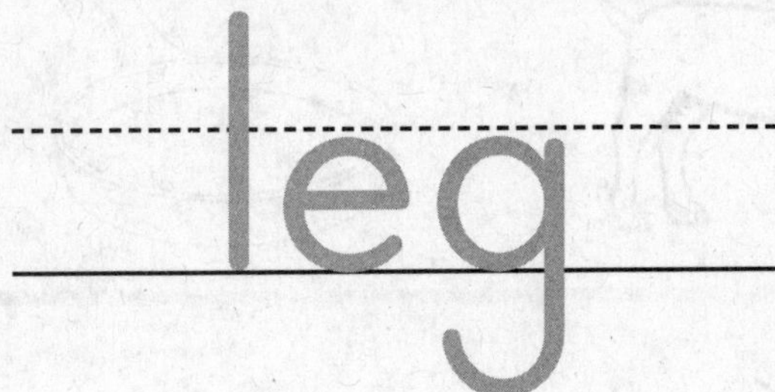

4. 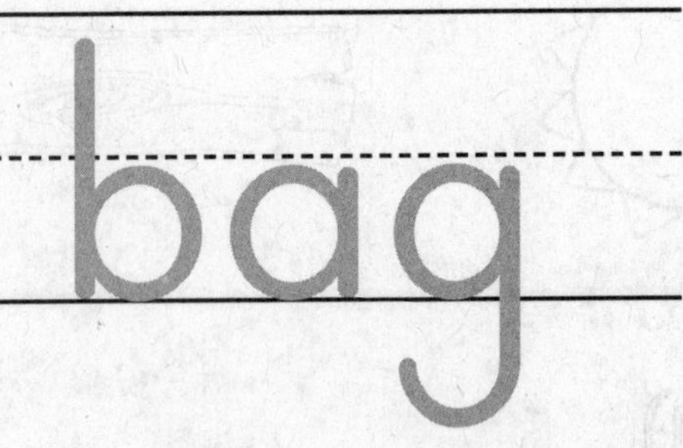

5. cab

Phonics: ***b*, initial *l***
Listen as I say each picture name. Then read each each word. Spell each word, tracing the letters.
Draw a line from the word to the picture it names.

Name ____________________

bed	lid	log
lip	cab	bat

1. 

2. 

3. 

4. 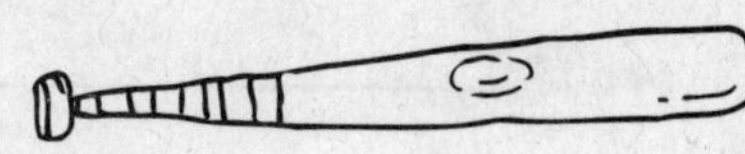

5. 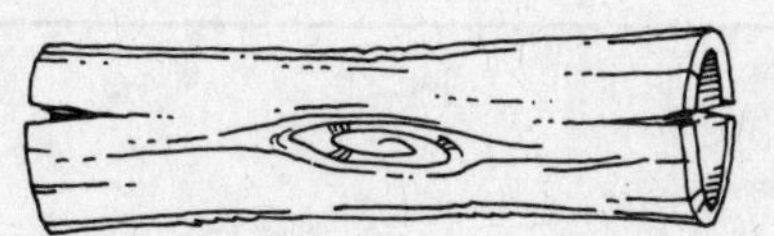

6. 

Phonics: ***b*, initial *l***
Listen as I read the words in the Word Box. Look at each picture. Write the word from the Word Box that names the picture.

Name ______________________________

1.

Nick is with Mom.

2.

Get a little pet.

3.

The ________ pet ________

________________________________.

High-Frequency Words: ***is, little***

*1.*Read the sentence and trace the word *is* to complete the sentence. 2. Read the sentence and trace the word *little* to complete the sentence. 3. Use the words *is, little* to complete the sentence. Then draw a picture of Nick's pet.

Name ____________________

Ben can sit.

Rob did not nab Ben.

Ben Ran

Ben had a little bit.

Ben ran!

Rob ran. Bad Rob!

Ben let it go.

Ben is at the top.

Name ____

1.

  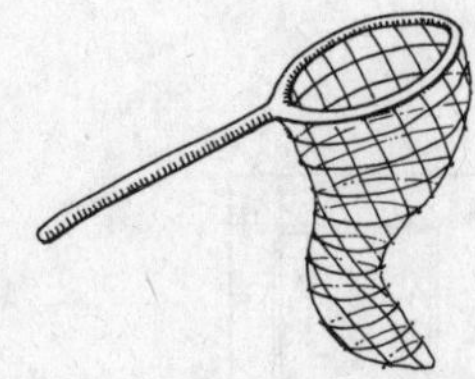

2.

3.

 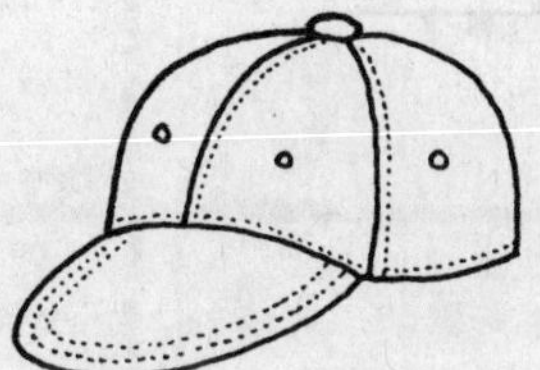 

4.

  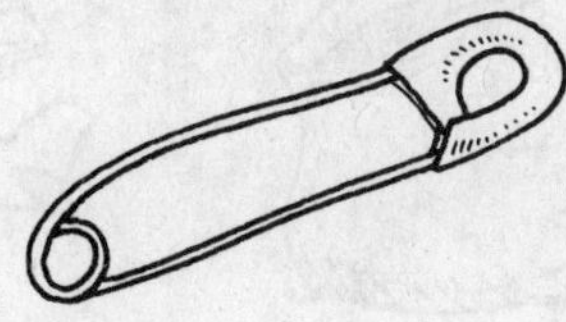

5.

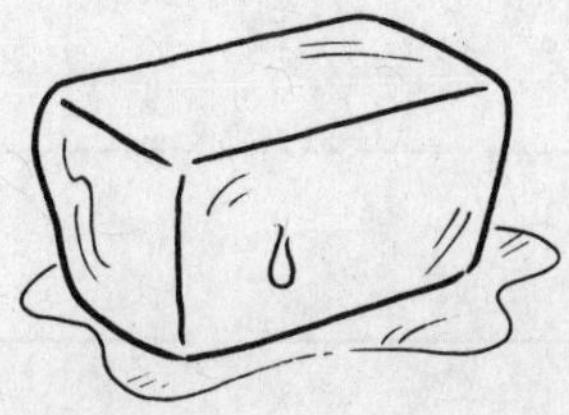 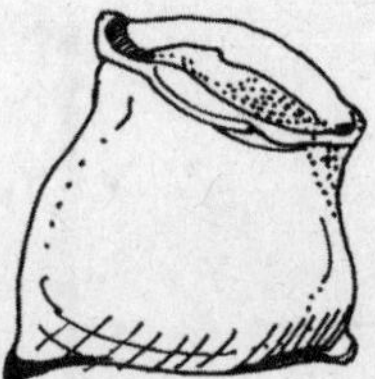 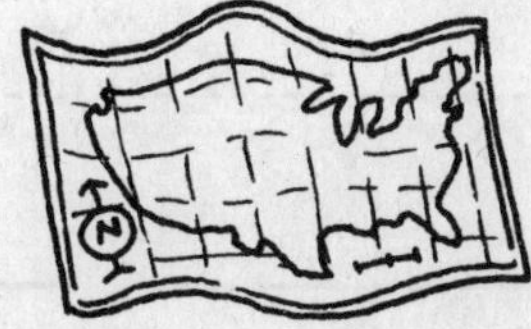

Phonemic Awareness: **Phoneme Isolation**
I will say a word. Then I will say 3 words. Circle the picture that names the word that has the same middle sound as the first word I say. I. sick; dog, kick, net; 2. mice; lid, fan, kite; 3. kiss; fan, cap, fish; 4. frog; lock, bike, pin; 5. fuse; cube, sack, map.

Name ______________________________

1.

2.

3.

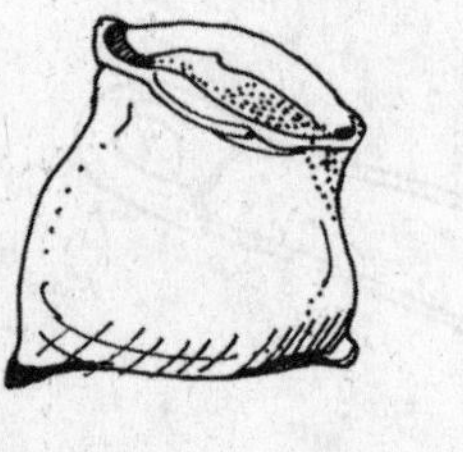

4.

Phonics: **initial *k*, final *ck***

1-2: Listen as I say each picture name. Circle the picture whose name has the sound /k/ at the beginning. Write a *k* on the line below the picture. *(door, kite; king, gate)* 3-4: Listen as I say each picture name. Circle the picture whose name has the /k/ sound at the end. Write *ck* on the line below the picture. *(sack, jet; flag, lock)*

Name ____

1. 

id

2. 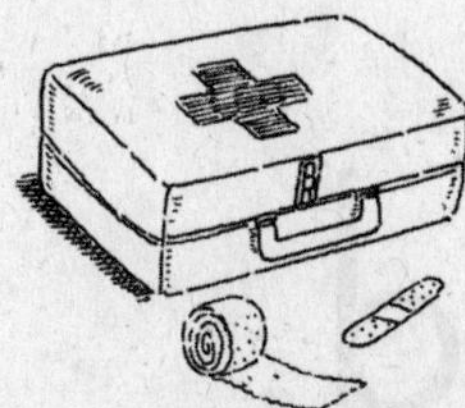

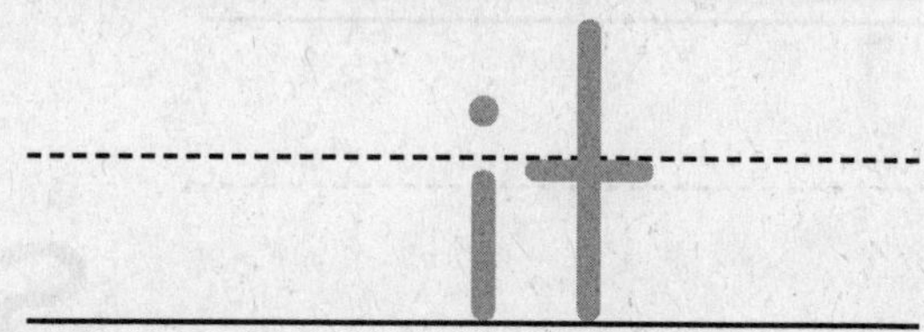

3. 

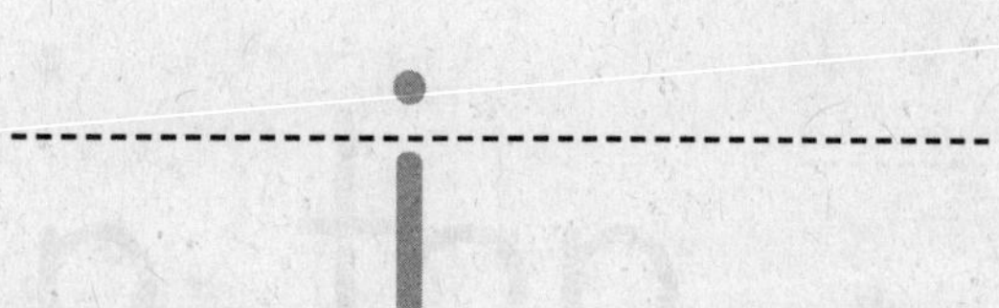

4. 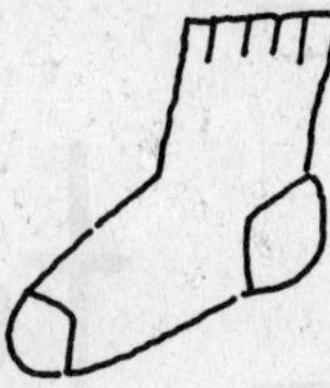

so

5. 

Phonics: **initial *k*, final *ck***
Listen as I say each picture name. Fill in the missing letter or letters for each word. Then trace the word. *(kid, kit, kick, sock, lick)*

Name ______________________

she was

1. Pam ________ sad.

2. ________ got a cat.

3. The cat ________ tan.

4. ________ had a pal.

High-Frequency Words: ***she, was***

Listen as I read the words in the box. Say the words after me and trace the words in the box. Now read each sentence. . Write the word from the box that completes the sentence on the line.

Name ______________________

Kit Cat was little.

Kit Cat is fat!

Kit Cat

Little Kit Cat can sit.

She can sit and lick.

Kim met Kit Cat.

Kit Cat can nab.

Nick can pat a back.

Kit Cat can lap.

Name ____________________

1.

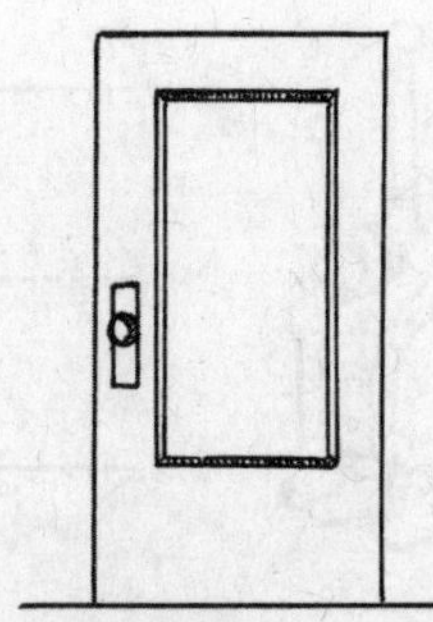

2.

3.

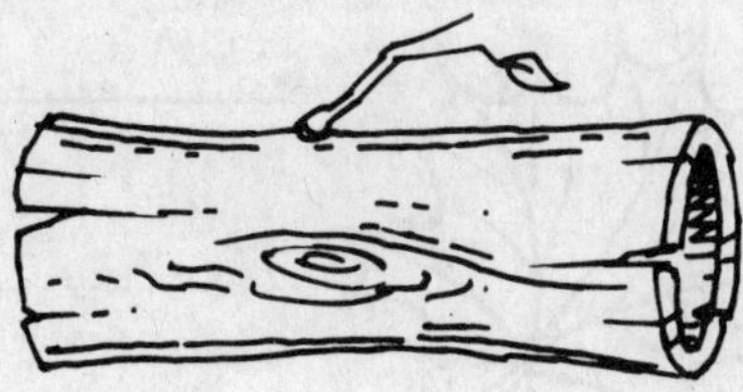

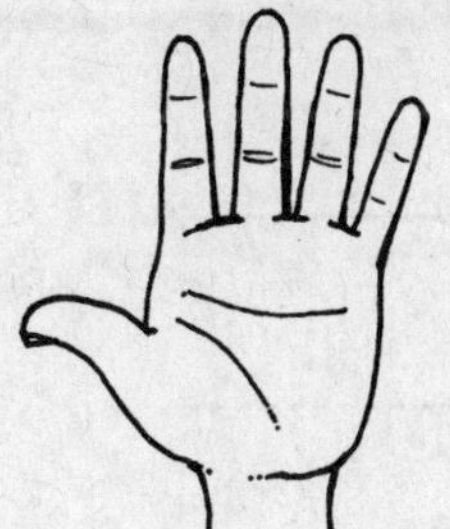

4.

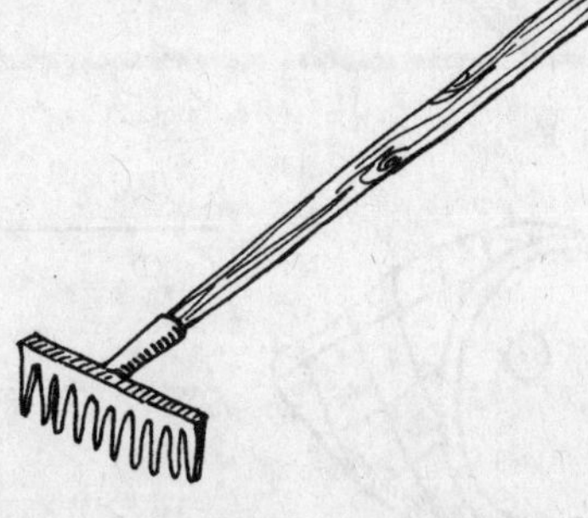

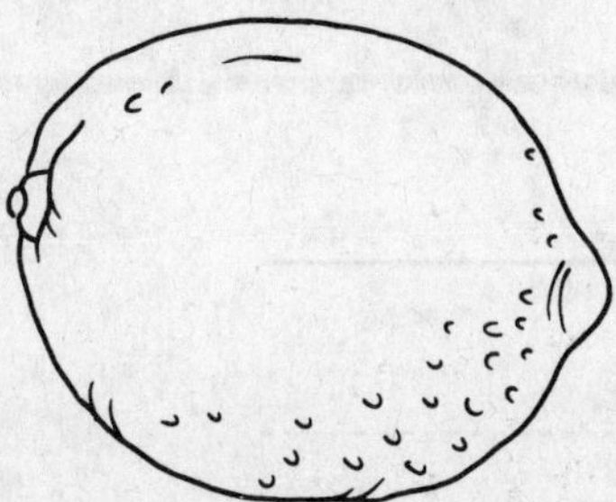

Phonemic Awareness: Phoneme Identity
Listen carefully as I say each picture name. 1. Circle the pictures in the row that have the sound /b/ as in *bat.* (*door, bike, boat*) 2. Circle the pictures in the row that have the sound /f/ as in *fox.* (*fish, fan, sun*) 3. Circle the pictures in the row that have the sound /h/ as in *hat.* (*log, hand, house*) 4. Circle the pictures in the row that have the sound /r/ as in *rabbit.* (*rake, lime, rope*).

Write

Name ______________________________

I.

2.

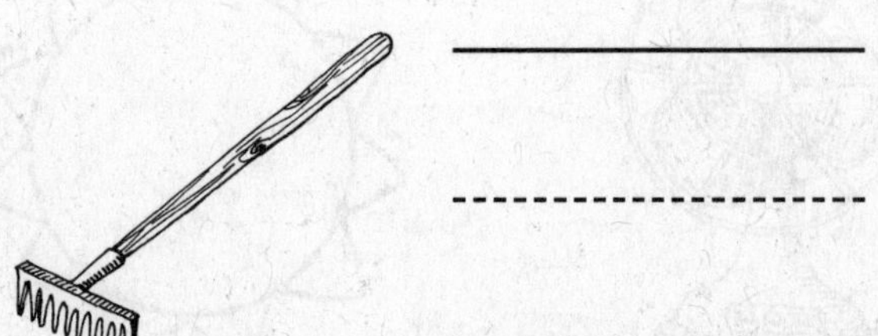

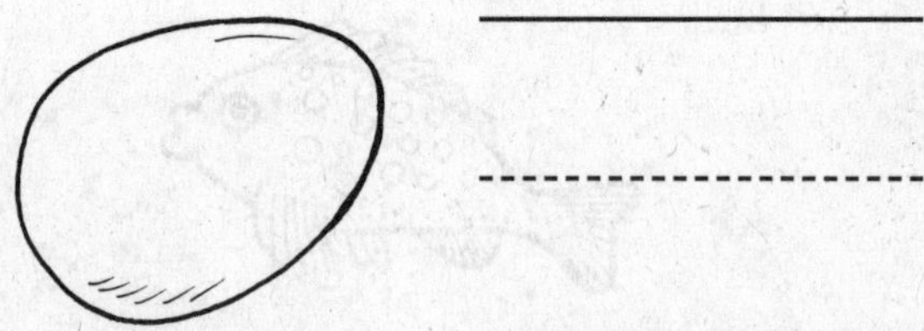

3.

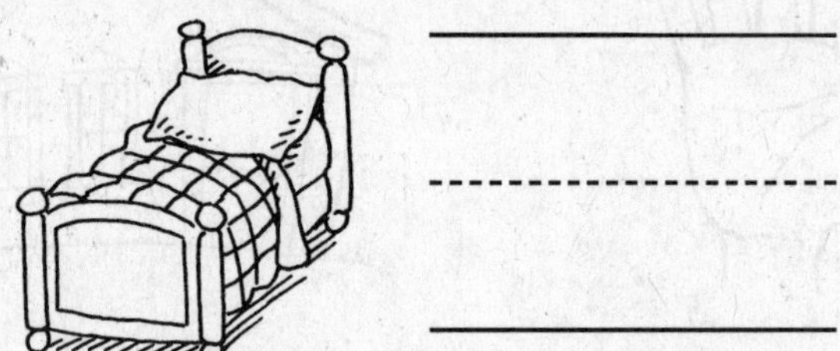

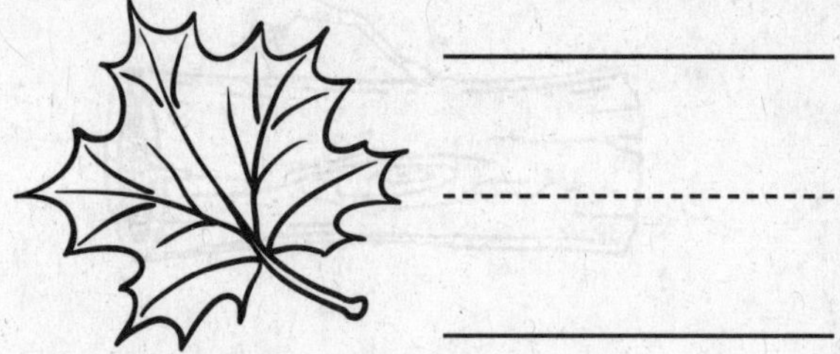

4.

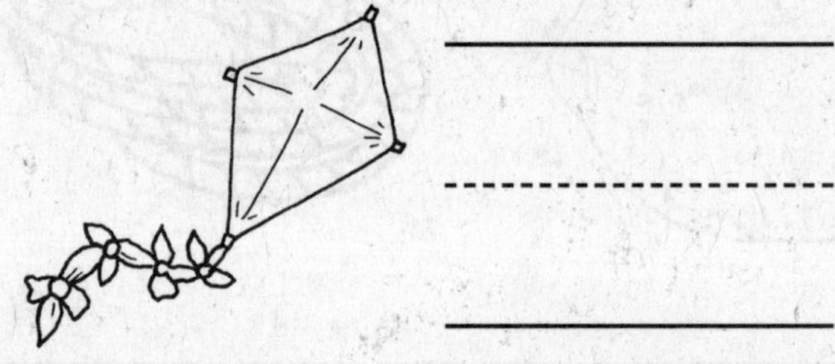

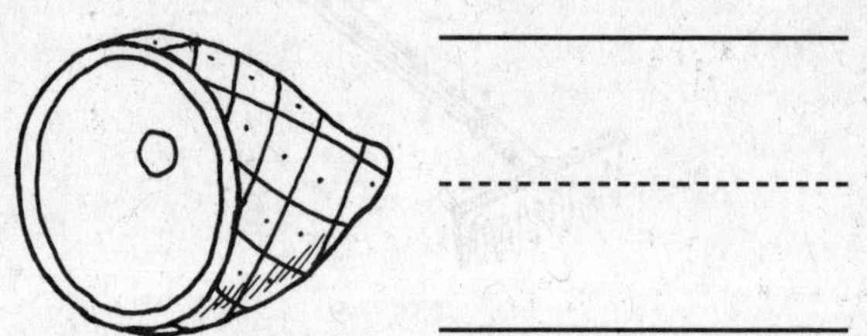

Phonics: short *e, h, f, l, r, b, k, ck*
Listen as I say each picture name. Write the letter that each picture name begins with.
(*fan, king, rake, egg, bed, leaf, kite, ham*)

Name ______________________________

bib hen kick lock

1.

2.

3.

4.

Phonics: short *e, h, f, l, r, b, k, ck*
Listen as I say each picture name. Write a word from the box to name each picture.
(*hen, kick, lock, bib*)

Name ________________________________

are is little my
she was with

1. Are Ted and

Kim with Deb?

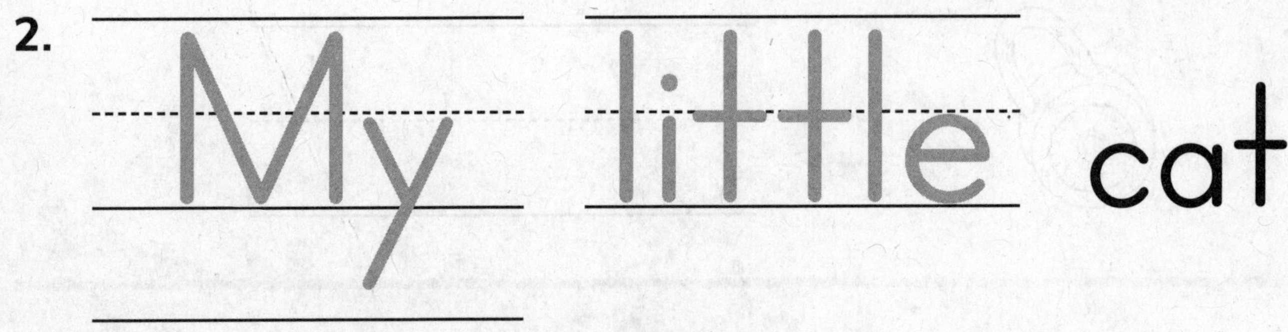

2. My little cat

was fat.

High-Frequency Words: ***are, he, is, little, my, she, was, with***
Let's read the words in the box together. Now trace the words in the box and then read them.
Read each sentence with me. Write a word from the box on each line to complete the sentences.

Name ______________________

Rick did not like it!

Kim did like it!

Kim and Rick Go!

Can Kim and Rick Fit?

Kim can sit in back.

Kim is with Rick.

She fit on the back.

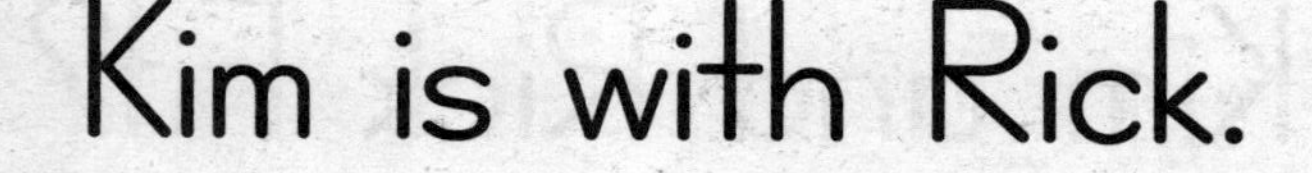

It was not bad.

Rick can go a little!

Name ____

1.

2.

3.

4.

5.

Phonemic Awareness: **Phoneme Isolation**
Listen carefully. I will say the name of the first picture, then I will say the names of the other two pictures. Circle the image with the same middle sound as the name of the first picture. 1. ten; bed, tub 2. hug; hut, cap 3. leaf; log, feet 4. glass; map, steak 5. pen; pet, pig.

Name ________________________________

1.

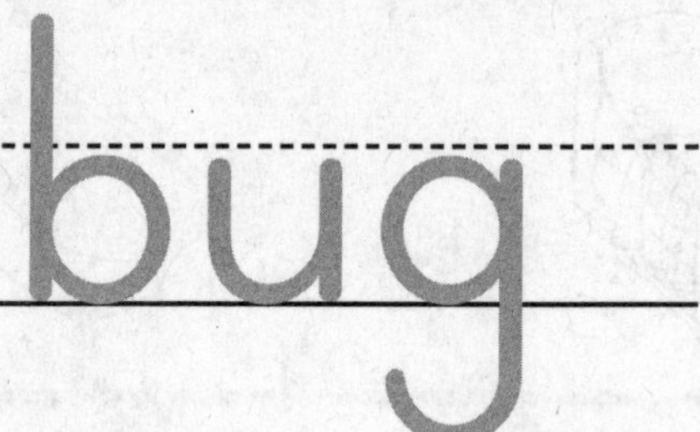

2.

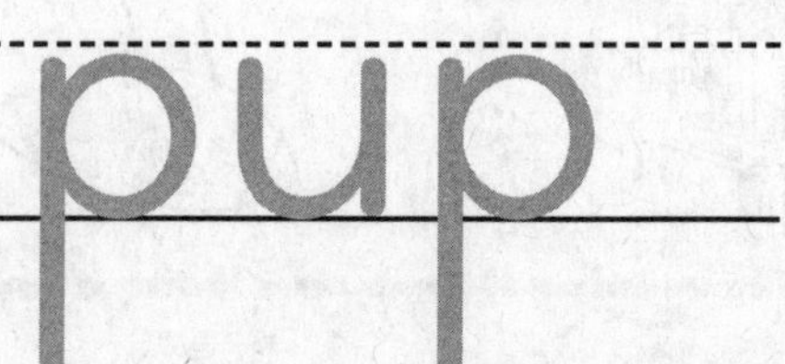

3.

4.

5.

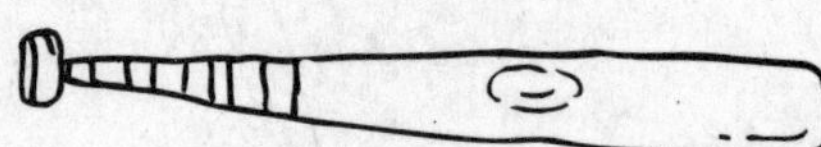

Phonics: **short *u***
Read each word. Then spell and trace the word. Then draw a line from the word to the picture it names.

Name ____________________

bus	duck	cub
sun	sub	cup

1. 

2. 

3. 

4. 

5. 

6. 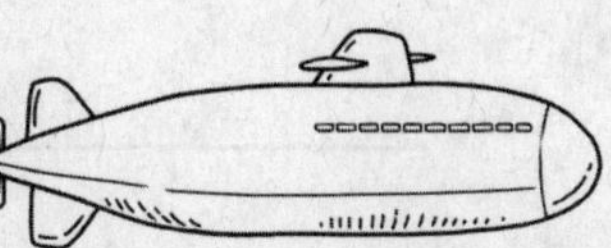

Phonics: **short *u***
Read the words in the box. Write a word from the box to name each picture.

Name ______________________________

1.

We run for fun.

2.

A pup is ________ Al.

3.

We have a bus.

4.

We ________ fun.

High-Frequency Words: ***for, have*** 1. Read the sentence. Say and trace the word *for.* 2. With a partner, read the sentence. Complete the sentence with the word *for.* 3. Read the sentence. Say and trace the word *have.* 4. With a partner, read the sentence. Complete the sentence with the word *have.*

Name ______________________

Rick is not in the tub.

Rick can mop it up.

Tub For Fun

Rick can dip in the tub.

Rick can have fun in it.

Rick can dip a sub.

Rick can dip it in.

Rick can pick Duck.

Rick can have fun.

Circle

Name ____

1\.

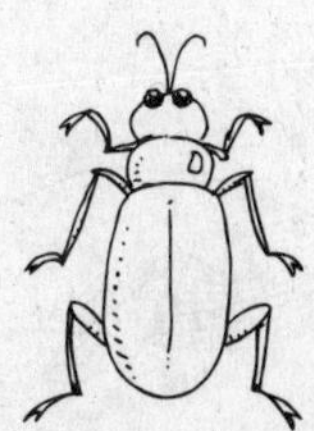

2\.

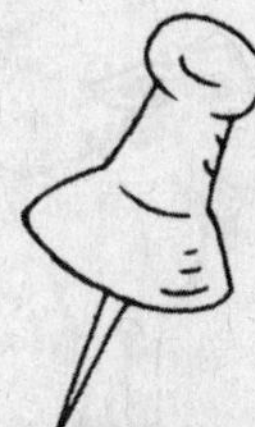

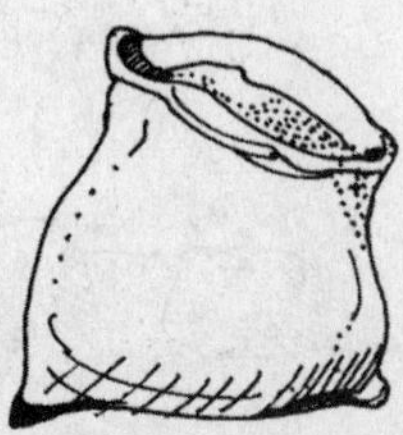

3\.

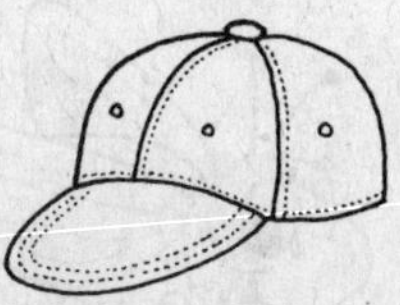

4\.

5\.

Phonemic Awareness: **Phoneme Isolation**
I will say a word; listen for the beginning sound. Then listen to the two choices. Circle the word that has the same beginning sound as the first word I said. 1. rose; bug, rug. 2. toy; tack, sack 3. core; cap, read 4. sock; run, sun 5. loaf; rock, lock.

Name ____________________

1.

wig

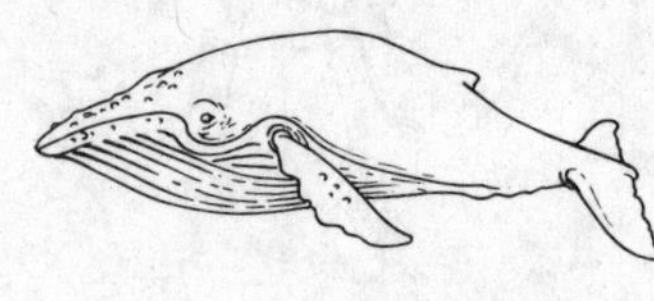

2.

gap

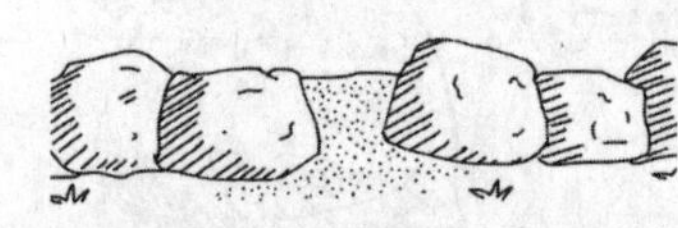

3.

bug

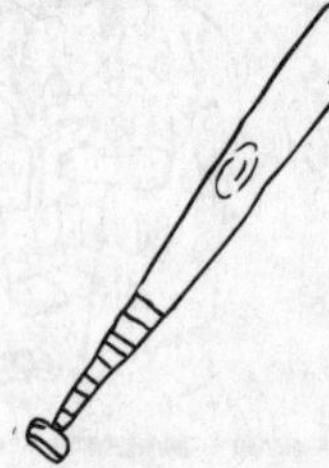

4.

pig

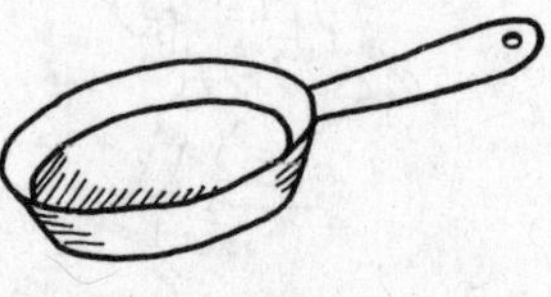

5.

web

Phonics: ***g*, initial *w***
Read each word. Circle the picture the word names.

Name ______________________________

1. 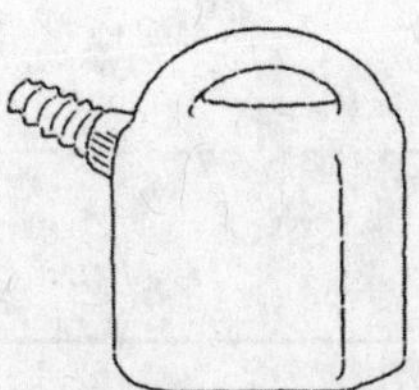

as

2. 

ap

3. 

do

4. 

i

5. 

eb

Phonics: ***g*, initial *w***

Listen as I say each picture name. Fill in the missing letter or letters for each word. Then trace the word. *(gas, gap, dog, wig, web)*

Name ____________________

they	of

1\. ____________ will go.

2\. Get a can ______ ham.

3\. Gus is a lot ______ fun.

4\. ____________ will go back.

High-Frequency Words: ***they, of***
Read the words in the box with me and then trace them. Write the word from the box that completes each sentence.

Name ______________________

Peg Pig is not wet.

They got to big rock!

Gus Rat Can

Gus and Peg sat.

Let us get to Big Rock!

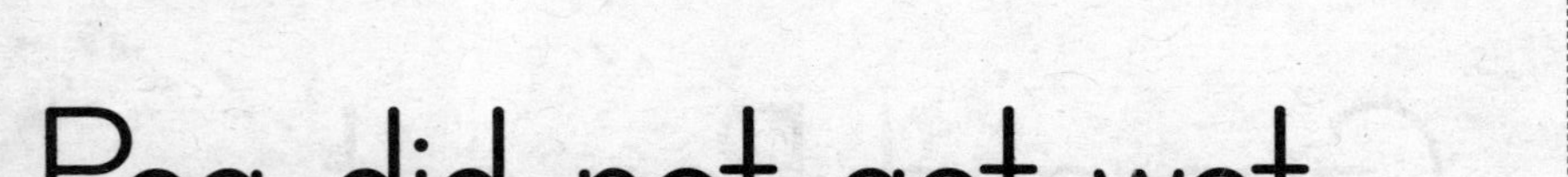

Peg did not get wet.

Peg Pig can not.

Gus Rat can get wet.

Peg Pig can get on.

Name ______________________________

I.

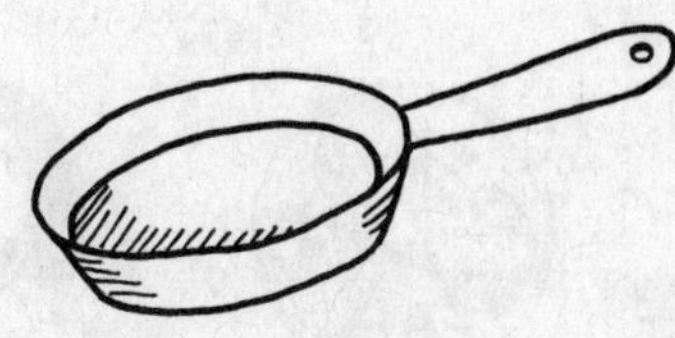

2.

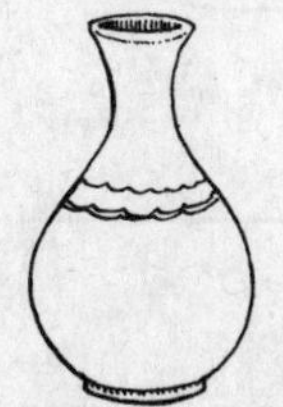

3.

4.

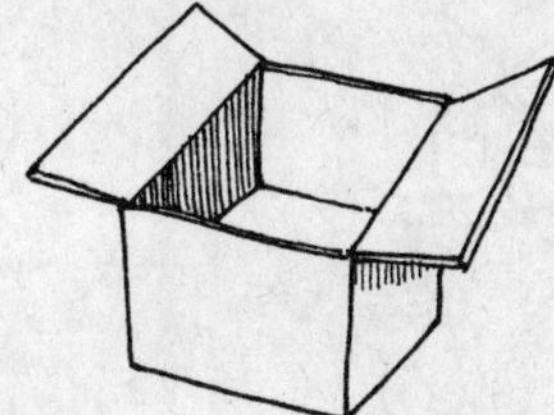

5.

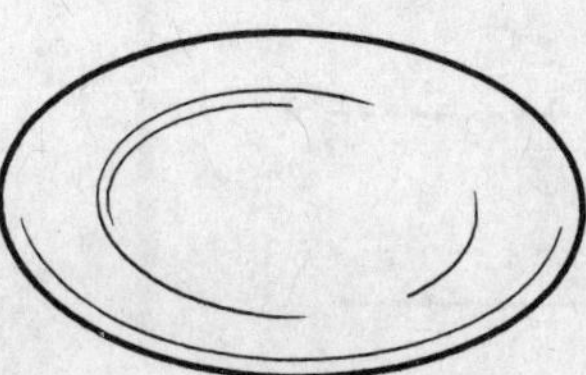

Phonemic Awareness: Phoneme Isolation
Listen carefully as I say each picture name. I., 2., and 3. Circle the pictures that begin with /v/. (*van, man, pan; cat, face, vase; vine, five, rug*) 4. and 5. Circle the pictures that end with /ks/. (*hat, box, bat; fan, plate, fox*)

Name ____________________

1.

2.

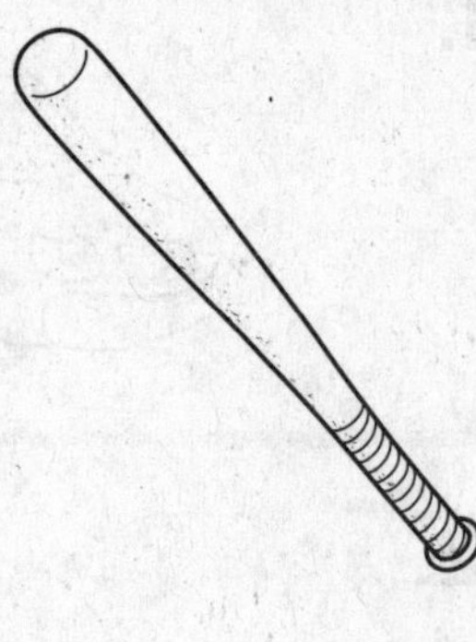

3.

4.

Phonics: initial *v*, final *x*
1, 2: Listen as I say each picture name. Circle the picture whose name has the sound /v/ at the beginning. Write a *v* on the line below the picture. (*fan, vet; veil, bat*) 3, 4: Listen as I say each picture name. Circle the picture whose name has the /ks/ sound at the end. Write an *x* on the line below the picture. (*ice, mix; ox, milk*)

Write

Name ______________________________

1. 

fo

2. 

an

3. 

et

4. 

si

5. 

bo

Phonics: initial *v*, final *x*
Say the picture name. Then trace the letters. Fill in the missing *v* or *x* to complete each word, and then read the word. (*fox, van, vet, six, box*)

Name ____________________

1\.

Max said it.

2\.

Dad ________ that.

3\.

I want a sax.

4\.

I ________  .

High-Frequency Words: ***said, want***

1\. Read the first sentence. Say and trace the word *said.* 2. With a partner, read the sentence. Complete the sentence with the word *said.* 3. Read the sentence. Say and trace the word *want.* 4. Read the sentence. Write the word *want.* Draw a picture of something you want to complete the sentence.

Name ____________________

Vet Lex sat.

"I want a nap!"

Vet Lex Can Fix It!

Cat and Rex are sick.

Lex said, "I can fix it!"

Big Rex bit it.

"I can fix it," said Lex.

Cat sat up on top.

Vet Lex can fix it.

Name ______________________________

1.

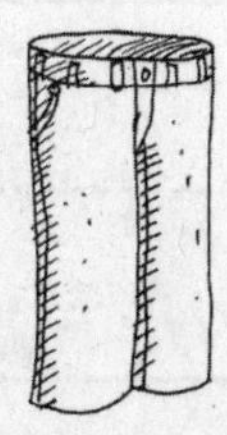 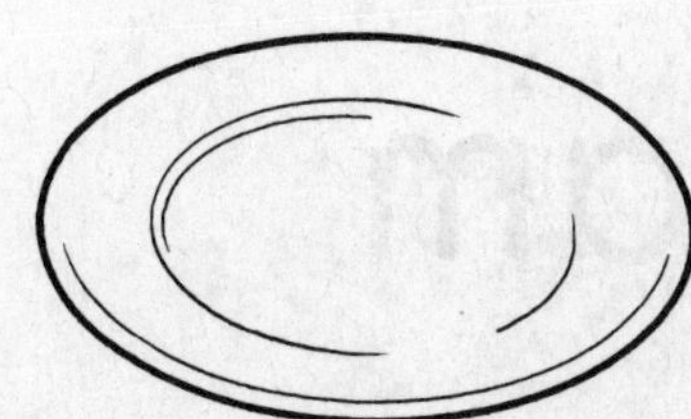 

2.

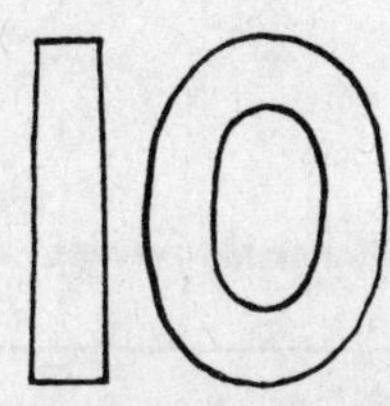  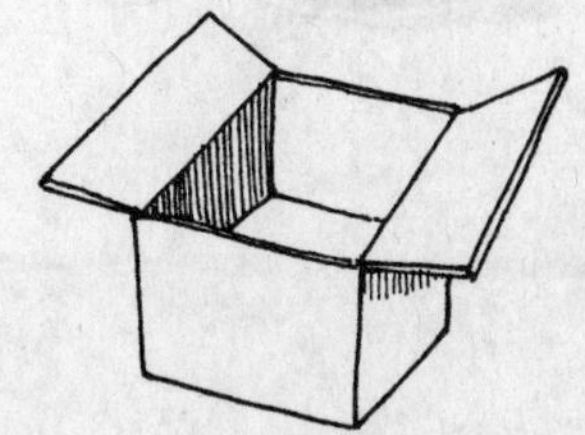

3.

4.

5.

Phonemic Awareness: Phoneme Isolation
Listen carefully as I say each picture name. 1., 2., 3., Circle the picture that begins with /j/. (*jeans, plate, fox; ten, jar, box; rope, heart, jet*) 4. and 5. Circle the pictures that begin with /kw/. (*queen, juice, fish; dog, gate, quarter*)

Name ______________________

1\. 

jam

ham

2\. 

quit

quick

3\. 

quick

quack

Phonics: initial *j, qu*
Listen as I say each picture name. Circle the name of the picture. Write the word you circled on the line.

Write

Name ______________________________

1. 

ick

2. 

et

3. 

ack

4. 

am

5. 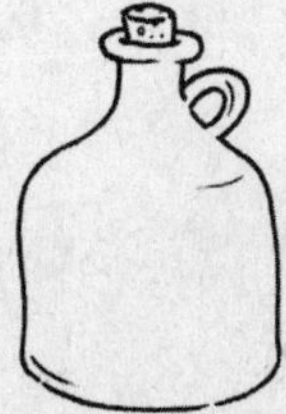

ug

Phonics: initial *j, qu*
Listen as I say each picture name. Fill in the missing letter or letters. Read each word. Then trace the word. (*quick, jet, quack, jam, jug*)

Name ______________________________

here me

1.

Jog with ________.

2.

We can jog ________.

High-Frequency Words: *here, me*
Read each word. Spell each word aloud. Trace the word. 1. and 2. Use the words *here* and *me* to complete the sentences. In the box, draw a picture of where you will jog.

Name ______________________

"Can you jog, Jack?

Jog with me, Jack!"

Jack and Jeb

Here is Jack Duck.

Jack can quack.

Here is Jeb Dog.

Jeb Dog can jog quick.

"Can you quack, Jeb?"

Jeb can not quack.

Name ______________________________

1.

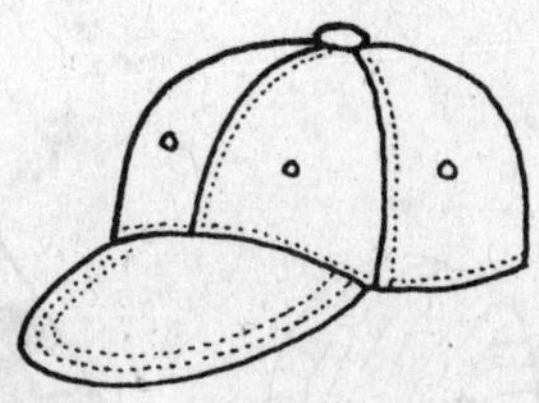  

2.

3.

4.

5.

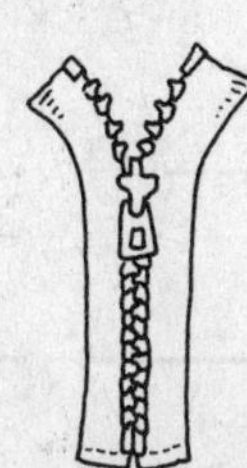  

Phonemic Awareness: Phoneme Isolation
Listen carefully as I say each picture name. 1. and 2. Circle the pictures that begin with /y/. (*cap, dog, yak; yo-yo, bat, fox*) 3., 4., and 5. Circle the pictures that begin with /z/. (*zebra, boat, tree; barn, shell, zero; zip, pig, bus*)

Name ______________________________

1.

2.

3.

4.

Phonics: initial *y, z*

I, 2: Listen as I say each picture name. Circle the picture whose name has the sound /y/ at the beginning. Write a *y* on the line below the picture. (*wig, yawn; yarn, game*) 3, 4: Listen as I say each picture name. Circle the picture whose name has the /z/ sound at the beginning. Write a *z* on the line below the picture. (*vase, zip; zero, sun*)

Write

Name ________________________________

1. 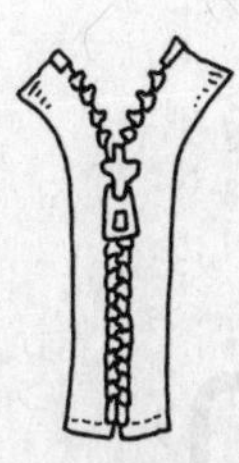

ip

2. 

ap

3. 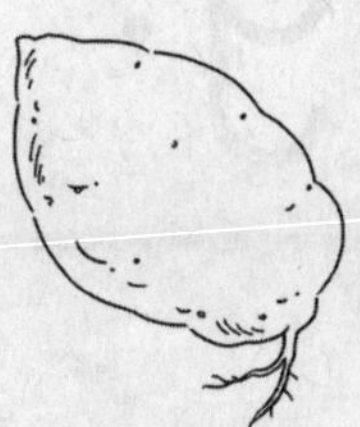

am

4. 

ack

5. 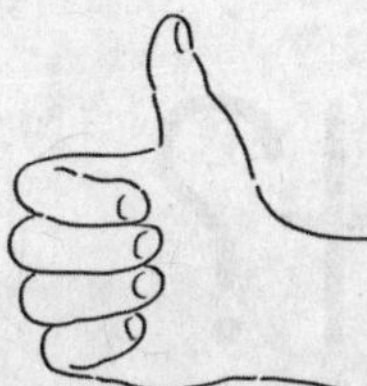

es

Phonics: initial *y, z*
Listen as I say each picture name. Fill in the missing letter for each word. Then trace the word. (*zip, yap, yam, Zack, yes*)

Name ________________________________

1\. This is a yam.

2\. Is ____________ a dog?

3\. What did Zeb do?

4\. ____________ is in it?

High-Frequency Words: ***this, what***
Read the first sentence. Say and trace the word *This*. With a partner, read the second sentence. Complete the second sentence with the word *this*. Read the third sentence. Say and trace the word *What*. With a partner, read the last sentence. Complete the last sentence with the word *What*. Remember to start a sentence with a capital letter.

Name ______________________

Zeb can get a hug.

Yes, Zeb can hug

Mom back.

Yes, Zeb Can!

This is Zeb.

What can Zeb do?

Zeb can zip it up.

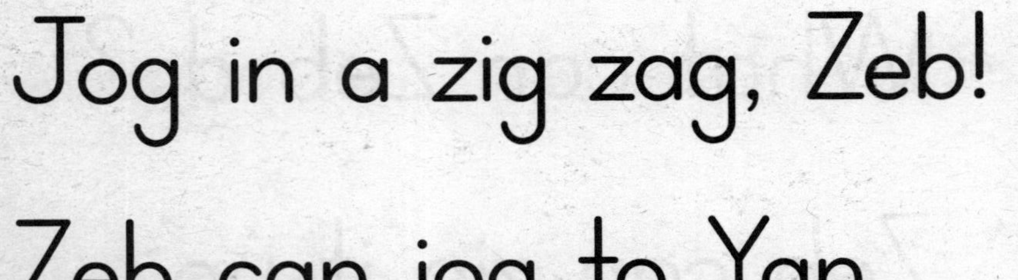

Jog in a zig zag, Zeb!

Zeb can jog to Yan.

Zeb can have fun.

Zeb can kick to Yan.

Name ____________________

I.

2.

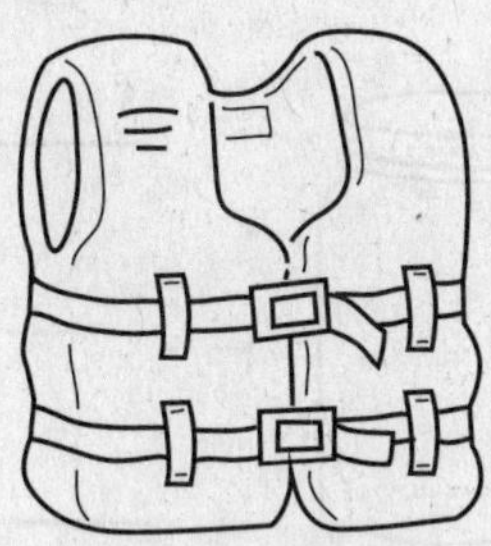
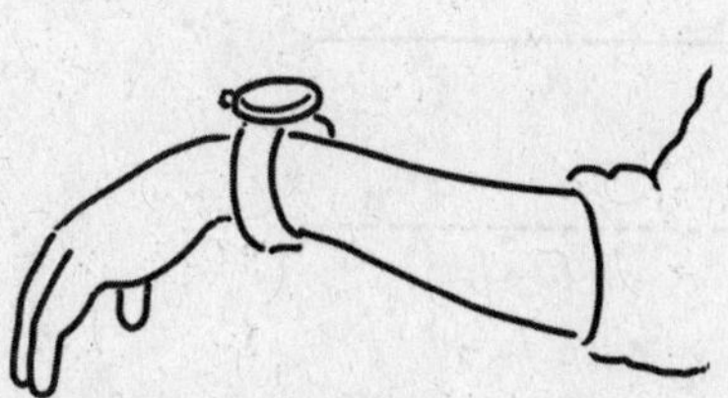

3.

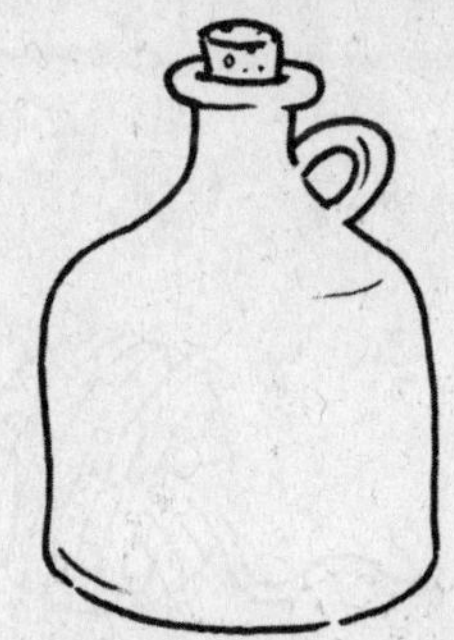

4.

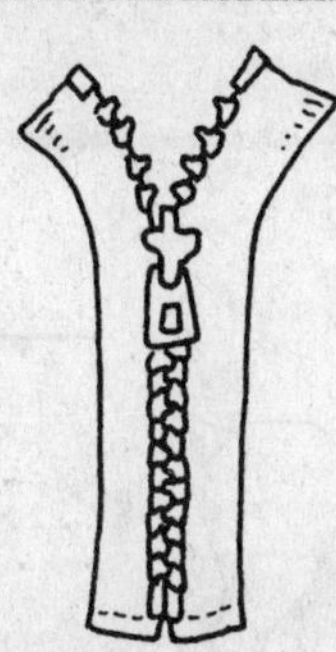

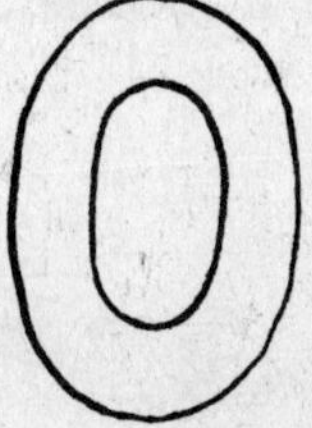

Phonemic Awareness: Phoneme Identity
Listen carefully as I say each picture name. I. Circle the pictures in the row that have the sound /g/ as in *game.* (*gate, goose, boat*) 2. Circle the pictures in the row that have the sound /w/ as in *wolf.* (*vest, watch, web*) 3. Circle the pictures in the row that have the sound /j/ as in *jet.* (*jam, queen, jug*) 4. Circle the pictures in the row that have the sound /z/ as in *zoo.* (*zipper, van, zero*).

Write

Name ____________________

1.

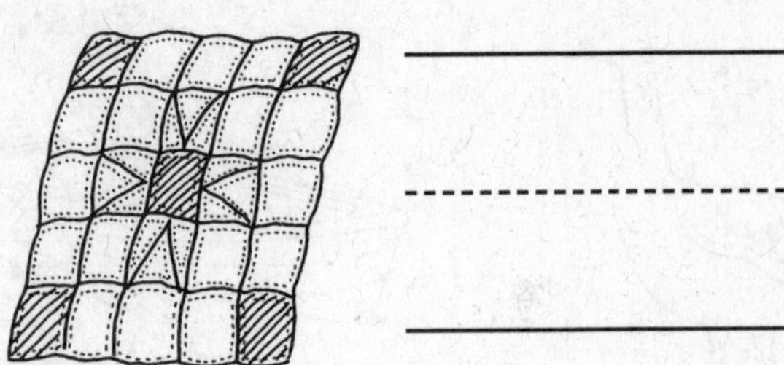

2.

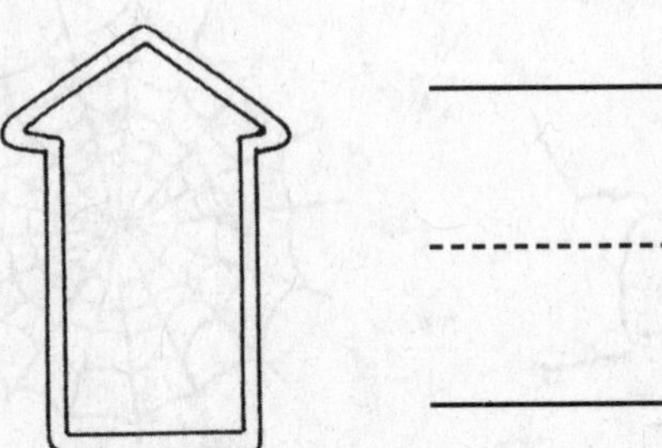

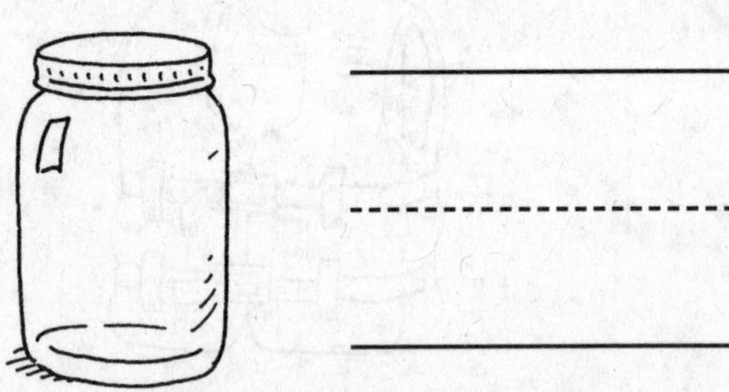

3.

4.

Phonics: Review short *u, j, qu, v, w, x, y, z*
Listen as I say each picture name. Write the letter that each picture name begins with.
(*quilt, wasp, up, jar, yarn, zebra, van, goat*)

Write

Name ______________________________

box jet wig zip

1.

2.

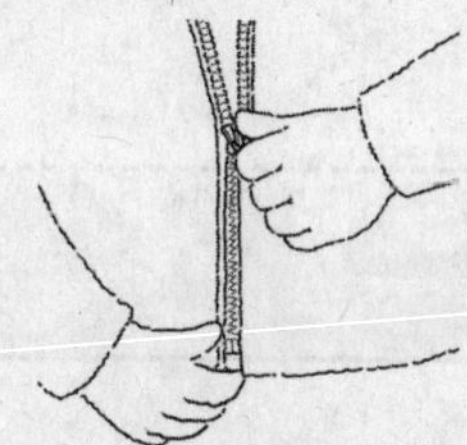

3.

4.

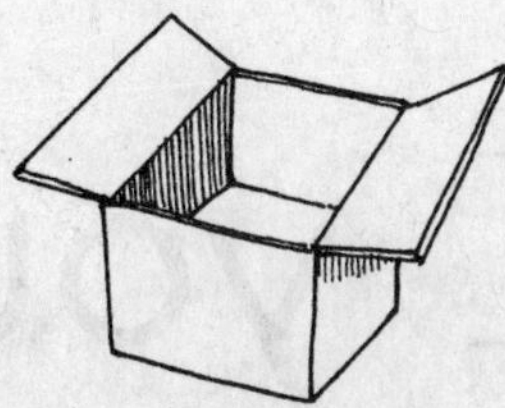

Phonics: Review short *u, j, qu, v, w, x, y, z*
Listen as I say each picture name. Write a word from the box to name each picture.
(*wig, zip, jet, box*)

Name ____________________

for have here
they this what

I.

They are here

to have fun.

2.

This is for you.

High-Frequency Words: ***for, have, here, me, of, said, they, this, want, what***

I.–6. Read each word. Spell each word aloud. Trace the word.

I. Trace the words *They, here, have* to complete the sentence. Read the sentence.

2. Complete the sentence. Write *This* in the first blank and *for* in the second. Read the sentence.

Name ______________________

Yes! Get a cat.

It can zig and zag.

It can get a big hug.

The Pet We Want

Vin and Jan want a pet.

"Can we get this pet?"

"It can hop in a box."

"Can we get this pet?"

"It can run quick!

We can hug it."

"Here is a fun wet pet.

It is in a big box.

It has a rock," said Vin.

Name ______________________________

1.

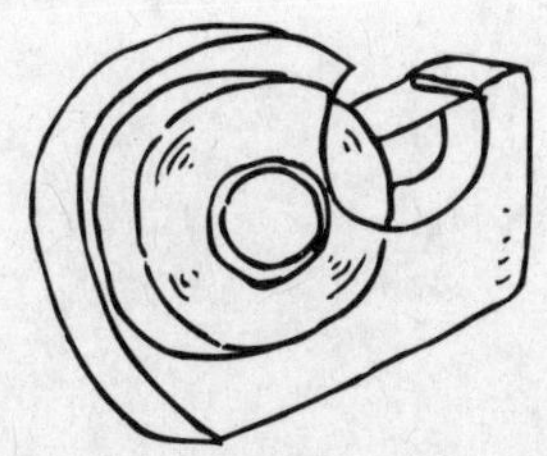 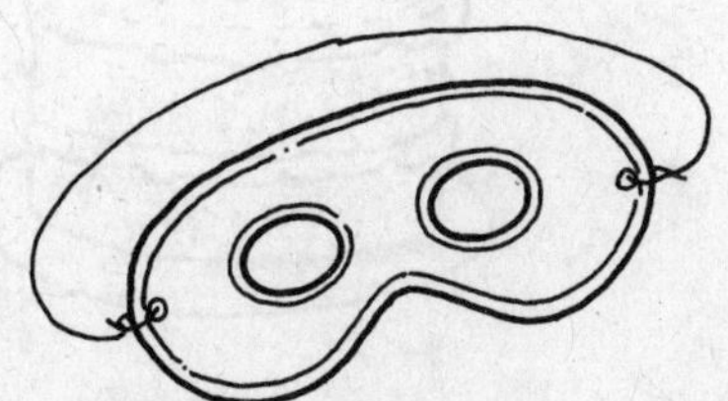 

2.

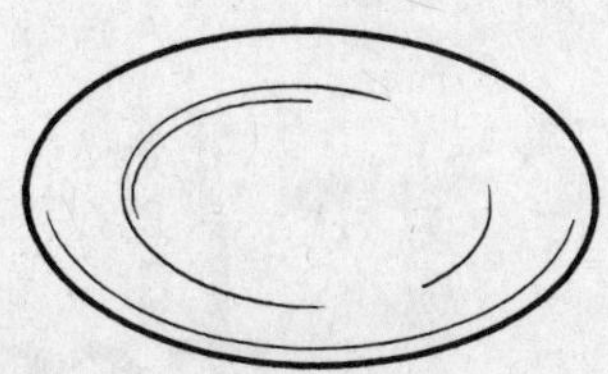  

3.

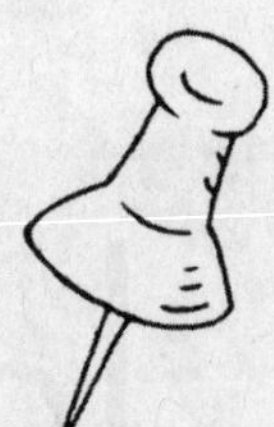 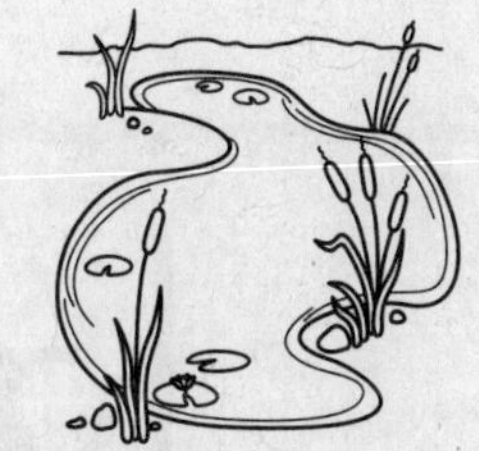 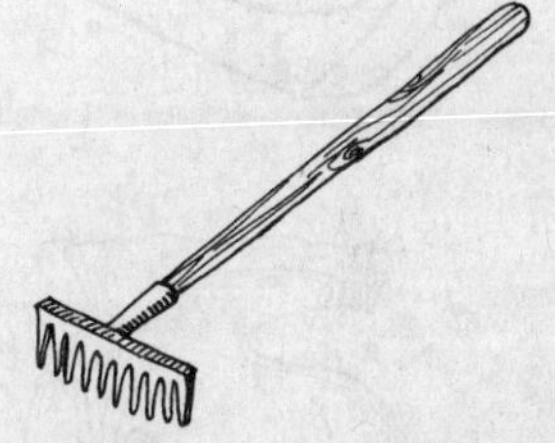

4.

  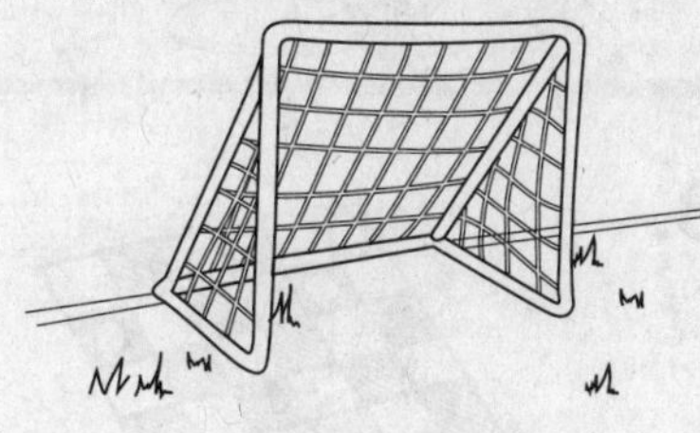

5.

Phonemic Awareness: Phoneme Categorization
Listen carefully for the middle sound as I say each picture name. Circle the pictures whose names have the /ā/ sound in the middle. (*tape, mask, gate; plate, plane, pig; tack, lake, rake; goat, game, goal; cat, cake, can*)

Name ______________________________

cake

1. 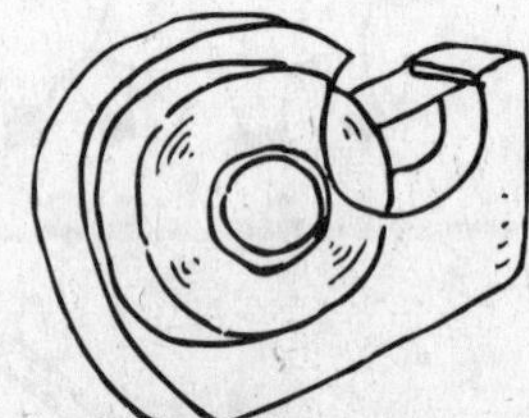 tap tape

2.  lake lack

3.  game tame

4.  rack rake

Phonics: Long *a*: *a_e*
Listen carefully as I say each picture name. Now read each word. Circle the word that names the picture. (*tape, plane, game, rake*)

Name ______________________________

I.

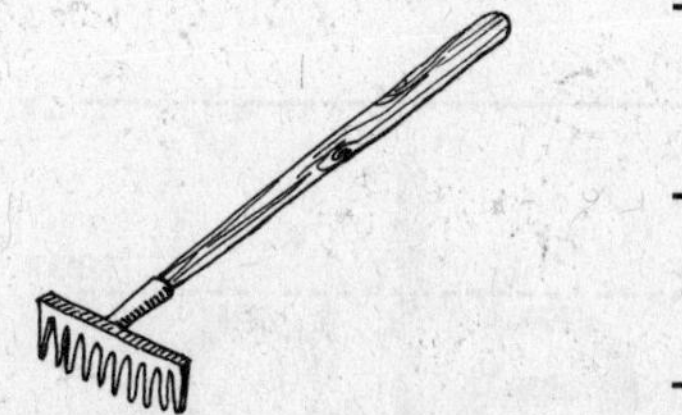

r ___ k ___

2.

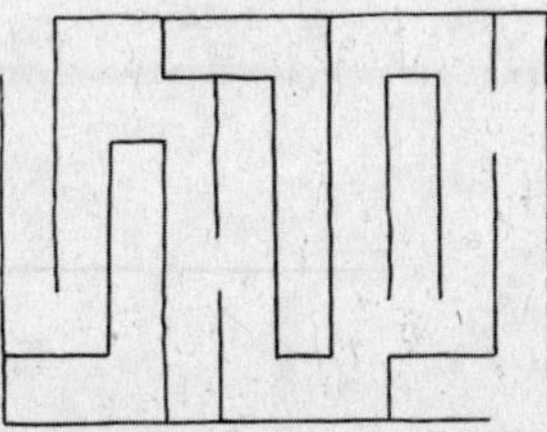

m ___ z ___

3.

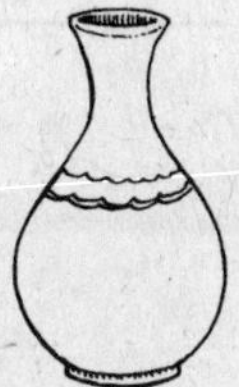

v ___ s ___

4.

___ p ___

5.

g ___ t ___

Phonics: Long *a*: *a_e*
Listen as I say each picture name. Fill in the missing letters for each word. Then trace and read the word. (*rake, maze, vase, ape, gate*)

Name ______________________________

1.

Gabe can help.

2.

Jane can help too.

3.

Can I help ________?

4.

I can ________ .

High-Frequency Words: ***help, too***
1. and 2. Read each sentence. Say and trace the word *help* or *too* to complete the sentences.
3. and 4. With a partner, read the remaining sentences. Write the word *help* or *too* in the blank.
In sentence 4, draw a picture of someone you can help.

Name ____________________

Abe can save it.

Abe made it safe!

Make It Safe

Abe came to help.

Can Abe help Kate?

Kate gave a leg to Abe.

Can Abe make it safe?

Abe can tap the base.

"Abe, tap the leg too."

Name ______________________________

1.

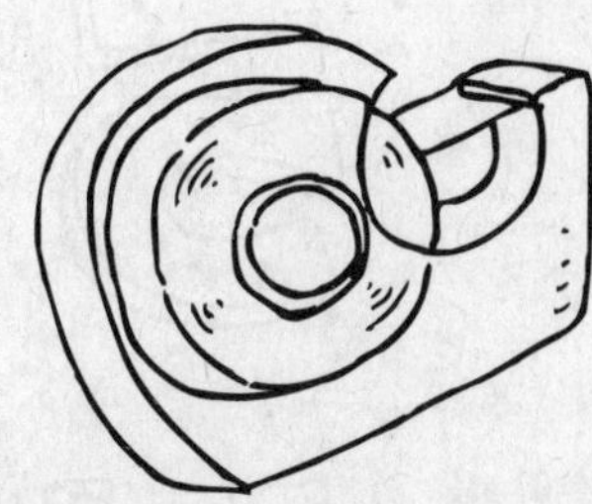

2.

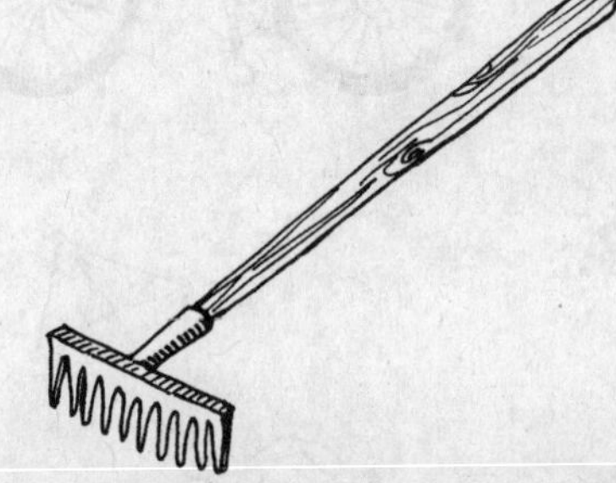

3.

4.

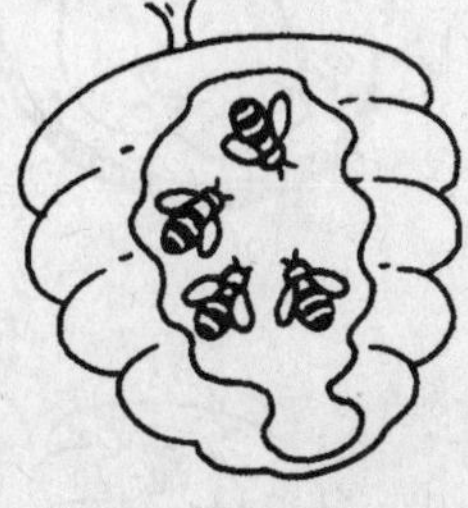

Phonemic Awareness: Phoneme Identity
Listen carefully as I say each picture name. Circle the two pictures in each row that have one sound that is the same. Then tell a partner whether the sound is at the beginning or in the middle of the picture names. (*bike, vine, tape; nine, dime, rake; kite, can, six; cape, slide, hive*).

Name ______________________________

1. 

kite

2. 

vine

3. 

hive

4. 

five

5. 

bike

6. 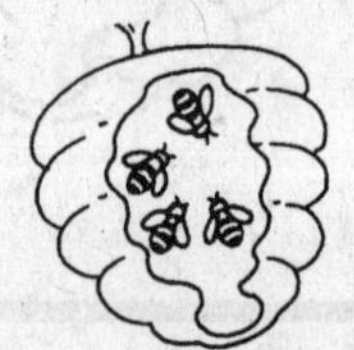

dime

Phonics: Long *i*: *i_e*
Listen as I say each picture name: *five, bike, kite, vine, dime, hive*. Read and trace each word. Then draw a line from the picture to the matching word.

Name ______________________________

1. 

b k

---

2. 

f v

---

3. 

d m

---

4. 

v n

---

5. 

k t

Phonics: Long *i*: *i_e*
Listen as I say each picture name. Fill in the missing letters for each word. Then trace the word.
(*bike, five, dime, vine, kite*)

Name ________________________________

has play

1. Mike ____________ a bike.

2. Gale and Rick ____________.

3. Jane ____________ a kite.

High-Frequency Words: ***has, play***
Listen as I read the word: *has, play.* With a partner, say and spell the words. Now trace the words. Read each sentence. Write *has* or *play* on the line to complete the sentences.

Name ______________________

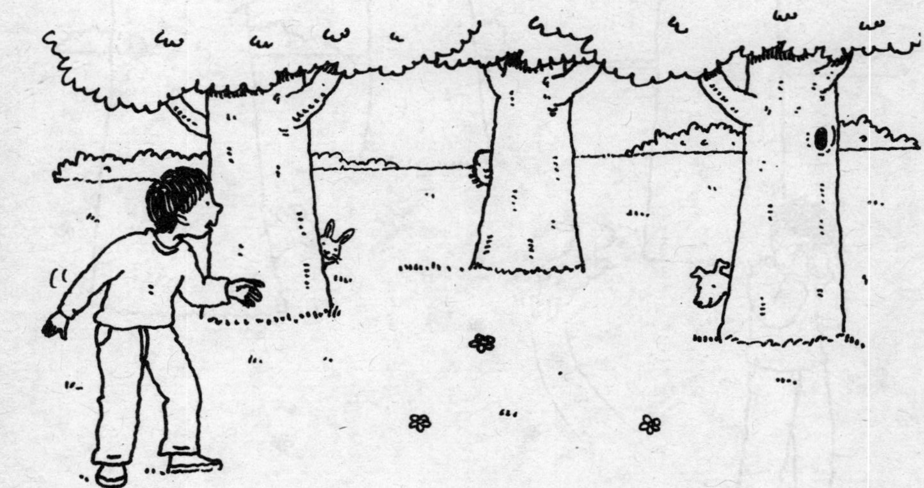

Mike has to get us.

Mike can tag us.

We had a fun time!

Hide Time

Let us play a game!

Mike can not see.

Jane can hide in back.

Ike can run.

Ike can hide on the side.

Pat can hop to hide.

Pat can hide in back.

Name ________________________________

1.

2.

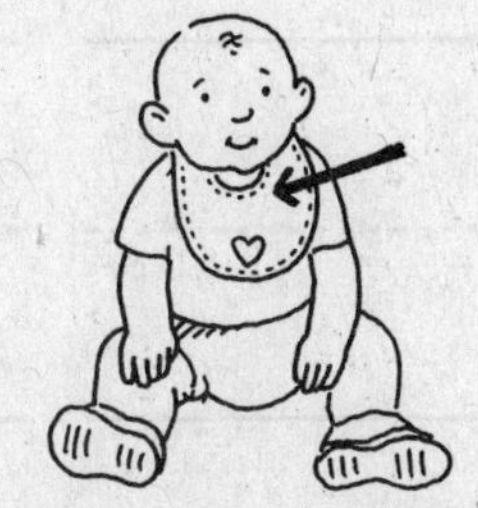

3.

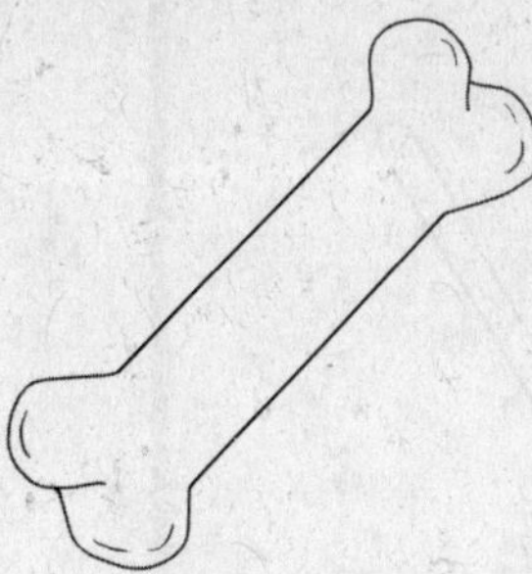

4.

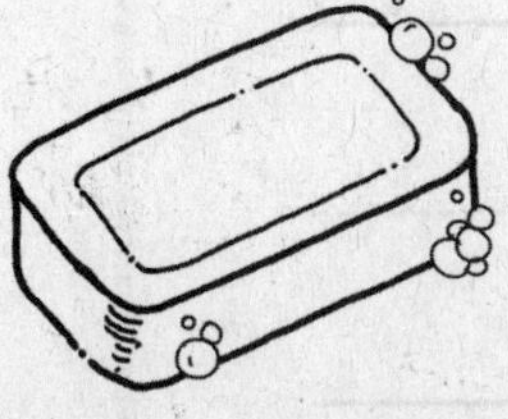

Phonemic Awareness: Phoneme Identity
Listen carefully as I say each picture name. Circle the two pictures in each row that have a sound that is the same. Then tell a partner whether the sound is at the beginning, middle, or end of the picture name. (*cone, mole, bee; boat, truck, bib; fox, bone, bike; rose, soap, book*)

Name ______________________________

1.

2.

3.

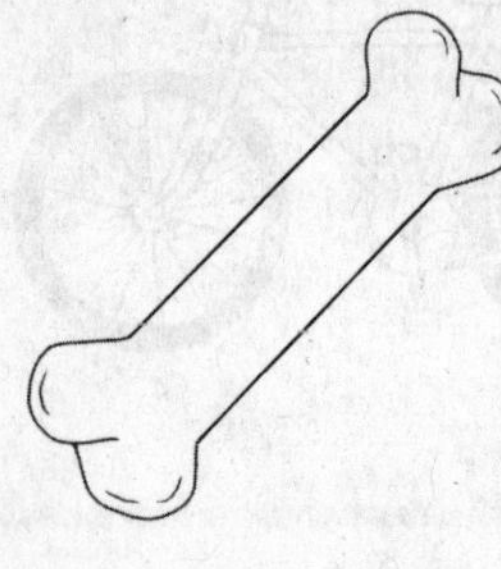

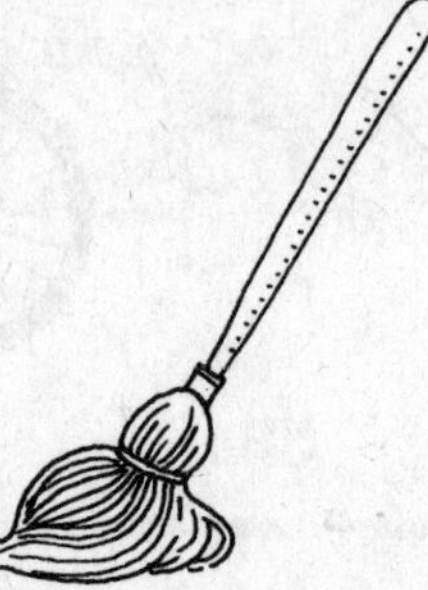

4.

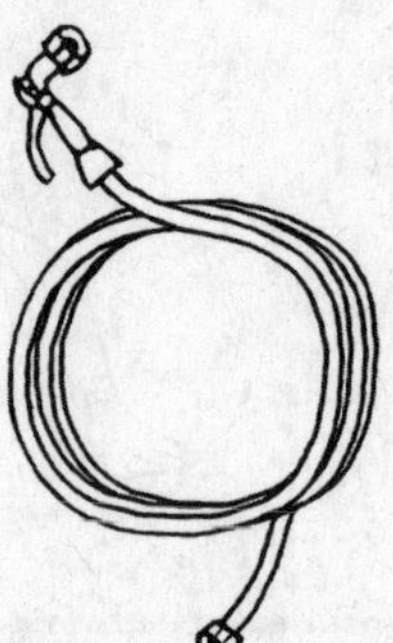

Phonics: Long *o*: *o_e, o*

Listen as I say each picture name. If the name has the /ō/ sound, write the letters *o_e* on the line. If the name has the /o/ sound, write the letter *o* on the line. (*globe, frog; knob, note; bone, mop; clock, hose*)

Name ______________________________

1.

r p

2.

c n

3.

h m

4.

p l

5.

g

Phonics: Long *o*: *o_e, o*
Listen as I say each picture name. Fill in the missing letter or letters for each word. Then trace the word. (*rope, cone, home, pole, go*)

Name ____________________

1\. Look for a hole.

2\. ________ for the note.

3\. Where was it?

4\. ________ is the dog?

High-Frequency Words: ***look, where***
1\. and 2. Read the first sentence. Say and trace the word *Look*. With a partner, read the second sentence. Complete the second sentence with the word *Look*. 3. and 4. Read the third sentence. Say and trace the word *Where*. With a partner, read the last sentence. Complete the last sentence with the word *Where*. Remind children that a sentence begins with a capital letter.

Name ______________________

Jo and Cole had fun.

Cole and Jo can doze.

Jo and Cole

Cole and Jo can play.

Where can they play?

They can play at a lake.

Cole can hit the pod.

"Get the pod, Jo."

Cole and Jo can look.

It is so fun.

Name ______________________________

1. 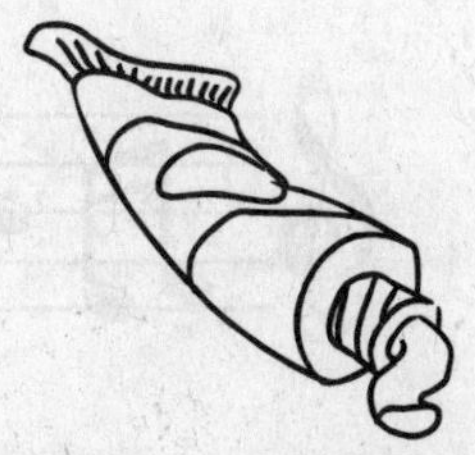  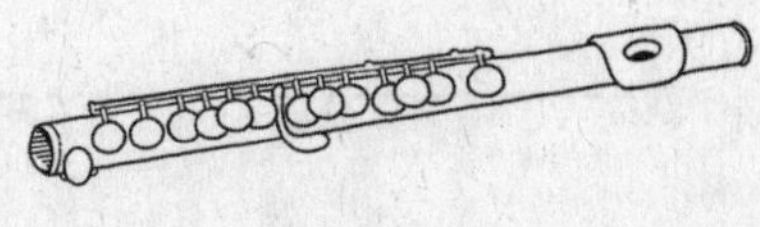

2. 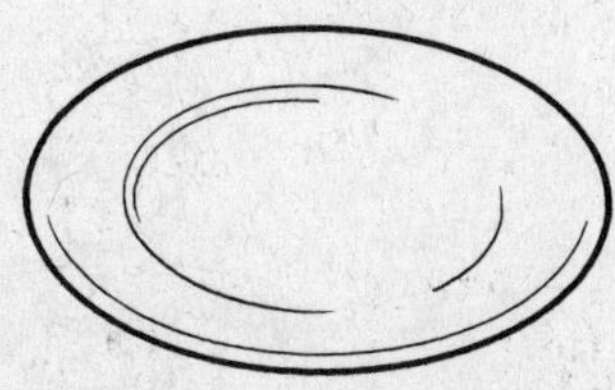 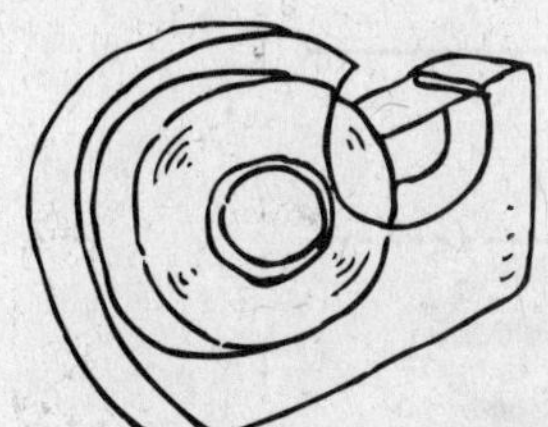 

3. 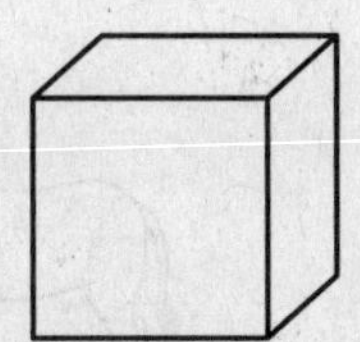 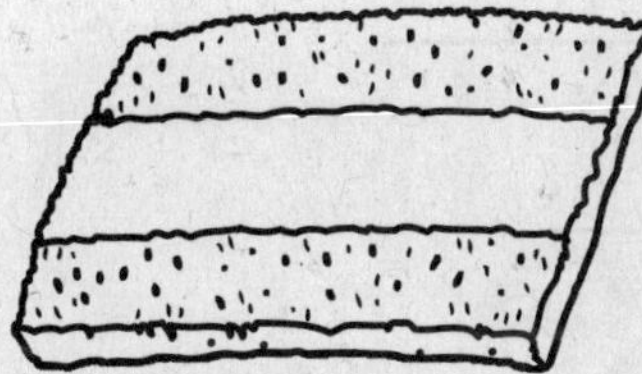 

4. 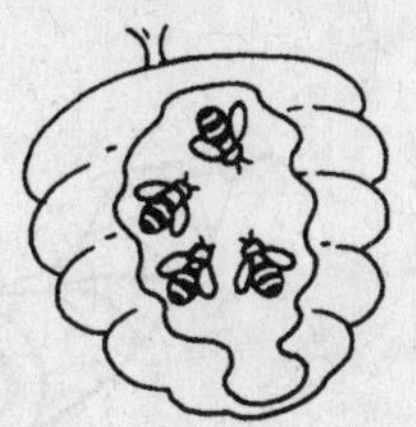  

5.   

Phonemic Awareness: Phoneme Identity
Listen carefully as I say each picture name. Circle the two pictures in each row that have a sound that is the same. Then tell a partner whether the sound is at the beginning, middle, or end of the picture name. (*tube, log, flute; plate, tape, mule; cube, mat, bat; hive, truck, five; dog, stew, duck*)

Name ________________________________

1.

2.

3.

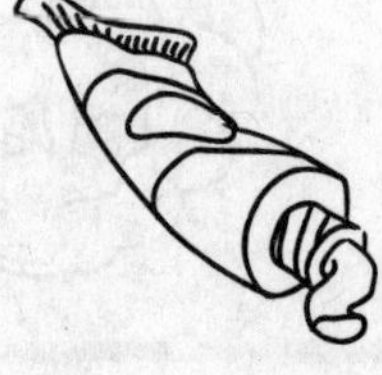

4.

5. duke

Phonics: long *u*: *u_e*
Listen as I say each picture name. Then read each word. Write each word, tracing the letters. Draw a line from the word to the picture it names.

Name ______________________________

mule tune cube
tube duke

1.

2.

3.

4.

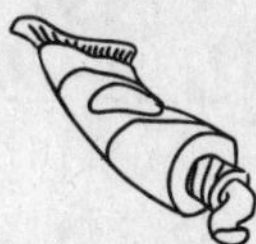

5.

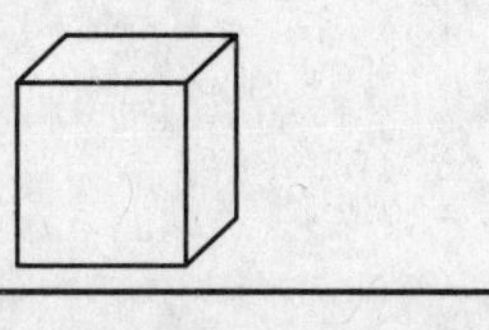

Phonics: Long *u*: *u_e*
Listen as I read the words in the word box. Look at each picture. Write the word from the word box that names each picture.

Name ______________________________

good who

I.

Joe is ____________.

2.

____________ can see a

?

High-Frequency Words: ***good, who***
Read each word. Spell each word aloud. Trace the word. I-2. Use the word *good* or *who* to complete the sentence. In the box, draw a picture of what someone might see.

Name ______________________

June, Luke, and Duke

can hop and run.

They can have fun!

June, Luke, and Duke

June can pat, pat, pat.

Luke can tap, tap, tap.

It is not a good tune.

Luke can hop.

June can hop.

Duke can hop too!

June and Luke run.

Duke can run too.

Who can win?

Write

Name ____________________

1.

2.

3.

4.

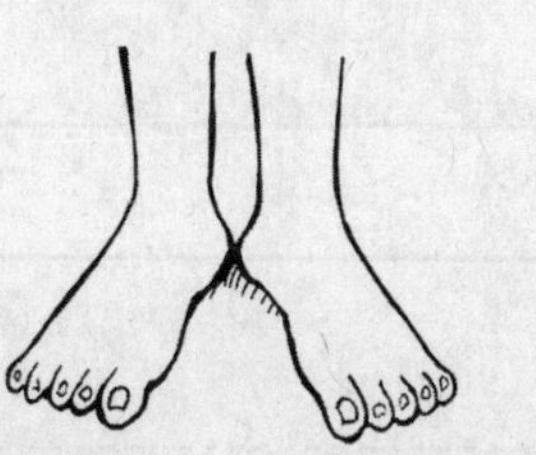

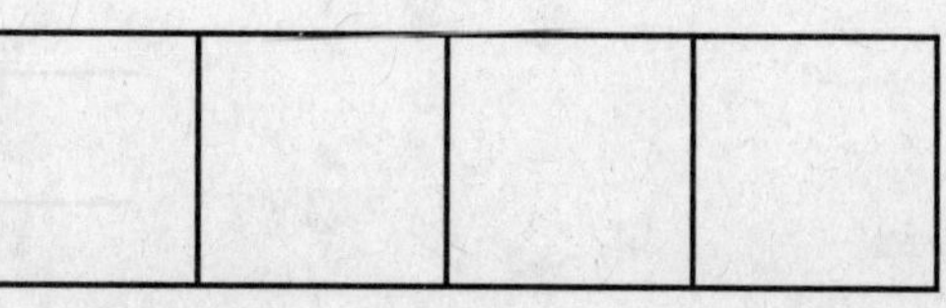

5.

Phonemic Awareness: Phoneme Segmentation
Listen as I say a picture name. Then I will say the sounds in the word, one at a time. Place one marker in a box for each sound you hear. Write the number of sounds. (*peel, bee, beet, jeep, feet*)

Name ______________________________

1. 

2. 

3. 

4. 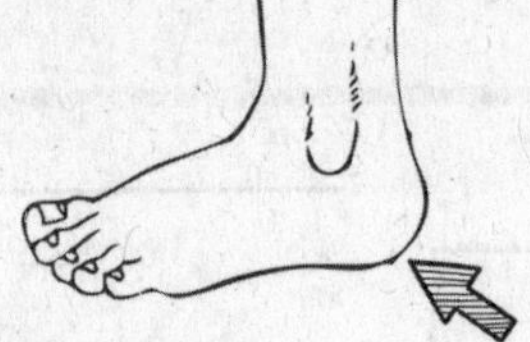

5. 

6. 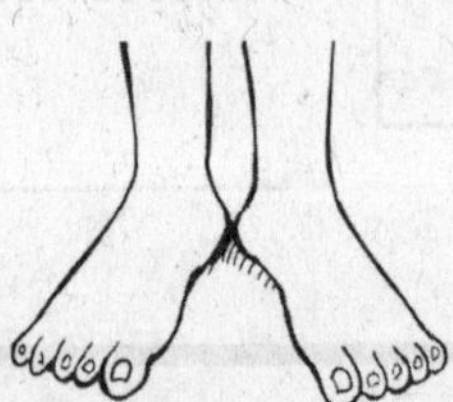

me

feet

jeep

beet

queen

heel

Phonics: Long *e*: *e_e, ee, e*
Listen as I say each picture name: *jeep, queen, me, heel, beet, feet.* Read and trace each word. Then draw a line from the picture to the matching word.

Name ___________________________________

1. 

qu n

2. 

m

3. 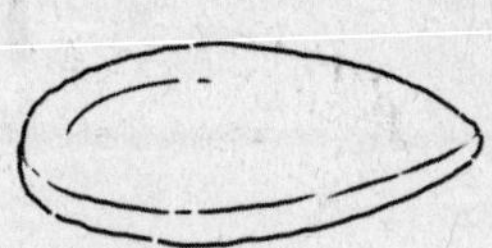

s d

4. 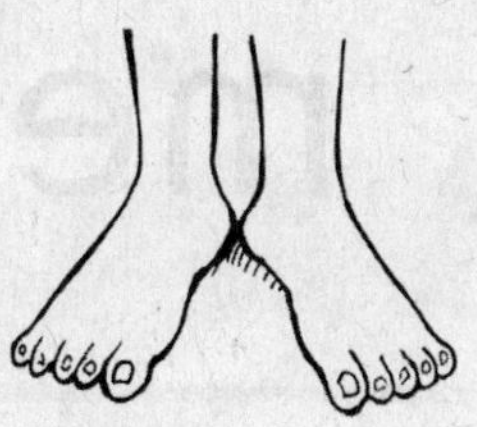

f t

5. 

b

Phonics: Long *e*: *e_e, ee, e*
Listen as I say each picture name. Fill in the missing letter or letters for each word. Then trace the word. (*queen, me, seed, feet, bee*)

Name ____________________

I.

You can come in.

2.

Can you ________ up?

3.

Does he see me?

4.

When ________ he go?

High-Frequency Words: ***come, does***
Read the first sentence. Say and trace the word *come*. With a partner, read the second sentence. Complete the second sentence with the word *come*. Read the third sentence. Say and trace the word *Does*. With a partner, read the last sentence. Complete the last sentence with the word *does*.

Name ______________________

Eve can tug on Pete.

Pete can tug the beet.

The beet does come up!

Big Ripe Beet

Pete had a beet seed.

Pete has a ripe beet.

Pete can keep it wet.

The beet is ripe.

Pete can tug the beet.

Eve can tug Pete.

Pete can tug the beet.

The beet did not come.